MW01195020

The *Evidence-Based* Clinical Quality Improvement Project Process Map

& Clinical Guideline Advice

Practical Guidance, Advice, Strategies, Tips and Efficiencies

Delfini Group Evidence-based Practice Series

By Sheri Ann Strite and Michael E. Stuart MD

"Best help with evidence-based medicine available."
Martin Gabica, MD, Chief Medical Officer, *Healthwise*

First Edition: May 28, 2015
ver: 20150824
Delfini Group Publishing: Delfini Group LLC
http://www.delfinigrouppublishing.com

ISBN-13: 978-1514127728
ISBN-10: 1514127725

Cover Design: Sheri Ann Strite
Cover Photo: Gerard van Schagen, Van Schagen's map of the world, 1689
http://en.wikipedia.org/wiki/Gerard_van_Schagen#/media/File:World_Map_1689.JPG

Table of Contents

What This Book Is About (And What It Is *Not* About...)

We Are About Improving the *Clinical Quality* of Medical Care

System improvement projects in health care are very important for many reasons: optimal use of resources, reduction of waste, respect for patients' time—and more. There are many resources that can help you achieve success with these kinds of projects. **But not this book**. Although, you may find some helpful tips here for these kinds of projects, that is not what this book is directed to.

This book is targeted to helping leaders, members and staffers of clinical quality improvement teams take the right steps, *efficiently*, to design, implement and evaluate an ***evidence-based* clinical quality improvement project (EBCQI) for a medical intervention**.

Further, this book is **not meant to address**, in depth, how to perform all elements of clinical quality improvement work. Here you will find advice that is useful for many non-evidence-based or non-interventional improvements; but this book is **specific to evidence-based clinical quality improvement activities with an emphasis on** *evidence*—although, at times, we will make a short departure such as a brief section on economic analysis. We tell you it is important to measure and report on clinical improvements, for example, but this book does not tell you the specifics of how to accomplish that.

As such, this book is very focused on the **quality of health care information and on optimal health care decision-making**. Having quality health care information *requires* an evidence-based approach. Thus, when we speak of **evidence-based clinical quality improvement**, we are referring to the use of *reliable* **medical science** to inform medical decision-making for **prevention, screening, diagnostic and therapeutic medical interventions on patients**.

To further describe what this book **can and *cannot* help you with** so that we are very clear: there are many resources that can help you do such tasks as getting the appropriate instruments to the surgery suite swiftly and efficiently. That type of quality improvement activity is **not what we do.** Our focus is on **whether you should be doing the surgery at all**. Which brings us back to the use of medical evidence—

An **evidence-based organization** is dedicated to identifying **reliable and clinically useful science** to help **close gaps** in such areas as quality, satisfaction and cost. When reliable science is **not available**—as is often the case—or when decisions are not informed by scientific evidence because of some other reason such as a regulatory requirement or medical-legal issue, an evidence-based organization is careful to be **transparent** so that users can differentiate between what is based on evidence that is likely to be reliable and that which is not (e.g., based on expert opinion or because of a requirement).

Evidence-based clinical quality improvement projects are usually **local** creations which include strategies, methods, processes, tools and information designed for a specific group or organization. When it comes to information, clinical content may be developed by the organization. Or, oftentimes, it is adopted or adapted from other sources such as clinical practice guidelines. And here comes another "should"—but **should you**? A key message of this book is the need for you to be judicious in your use of medical science because the fact of the matter is that **much of what you think to be reliable and clinically useful, is probably not**.

It may come as a big surprise to you that much medical science is not reliable, is of uncertain reliability or is of questionable clinical usefulness. This is a **key message** of this book. We want to make you aware of this—and we want to help you understand what you can—and cannot—do about this.

It is **beyond the scope of this book** to teach you how to determine if a study or source is reliable or not (although we have a wealth of freely available information on our website at www.delfini.org that can help you with this task). However, **what we will do** in this book is describe the problems with medical science sources in some depth; point you to resources that can help you with this, including how to tell if a person or group might be able to help you with the evidence-part of clinical quality improvement work; and, give you a structure and processes for EBCQI projects with practical guidance, advice, strategies, tips and efficiencies.

In this book, we provide you with our 5 core requirements + our 10-phase process steps for evidence-based clinical quality improvement. But before we go there, let's tell you another—and most important—**What This Book is About**...

We Are About the *Quality* of Medical Care; That Means We Patients

While you may choose—or need—to undertake an evidence-based clinical improvement project because of something other than a patient-centered issue, the patient should always be a vitally important consideration. And so our book is also about, and dedicated to, **patients**.

Information about the quality of the science should be the **right** of all patients.

A quality health care organization is dedicated to providing sufficient information to patients so that they can make decisions based on their own personal health care requirements. This requires a *true* evidence-based approach. The reason for this is that if the science is not reliable, the likelihood of accurately predicting an outcome drops.

Reliable medical science for interventions helps us understand two key things: 1) **cause and effect** ("Did taking this pill cause this outcome?"); and, 2) the **probability of an outcome** ("If I take this pill, what is my likelihood of experiencing an outcome?). Therefore, reliable (valid) science results in more precise **predictions of outcomes** for patients.

Patients **cannot give truly informed consent** without receiving information about the reliability of the medical science and the likelihood of their experiencing an outcome. Frequently, this should include **quantified information** conveyed in ways that patients can understand such as number out of 100 who are likely to experience a benefit or a harm—along with **external validity** information that addresses whether those probabilities are based on patients similar to them.

A truly patient-centered approach is one in which the individual patient—as a **unique person** with unique health care requirements—is at the heart and soul of his or her care experiences. This is what a truly quality health care experience is "about"—the person—not just the symptoms or the problem or the disease the patient presents with; not the provider's convenience or preference or limitations; not the machine-like, complex impersonal and de-personalization resulting from the "system" that the patient may fall into— but the patient, him- or herself. We realize that the realities are that a truly patient-centered approach cannot happen at times for many reasons. But a quality health care organization *strives* to achieve the ideal as much as possible.

This means that evidence-based clinical quality improvement projects that are undertaken with the patient in mind are developed with attention to accommodating the **personal health care requirements of individual patients**. This includes a patient's own personal health care problems, special circumstances, values and preferences, all of which go into informing his or her health care needs and wants. And yet, research shows that doctors frequently do not do a very good job of asking about individual patient requirements [Braddock]. An effective evidence-based clinical quality improvement project can help close this gap.

Other information patients rarely get; and which also is their **right**.

Patients need health care information that is—

1. **Accessible** at the time they need it;

2. **Accurate**;

3. **Understandable**;

4. Sufficiently **complete** (meaning that nothing that matters to them has been omitted);

5. **Personalizable** to them (meaning if it can't be customized specially for a particular patient, it needs to be sufficiently objective so that the patient can apply his or her own judgment); and,

6. **Usable** and **actionable** so that they can act upon it and apply it.

But often patients do not get this.

They also need **basic information** which includes information about all reasonable **alternatives**—including doing nothing—and the associated **benefits**, **harms** and other **impacts** including costs of all their choices. And often they do not get this.

Research performed by Braddock shows that doctors tend to focus on making treatment decisions, but frequently neglect key details that patients need to develop informed preferences and make informed decisions. Many patients want to know how likely it is that they will experience benefit or harm, yet frequently physicians don't offer information about benefit, harms or uncertainties. Often they fail in providing meaningful and understandable quantitative information about the likelihood of benefit or harm (and this research doesn't even address that when patients *do* get quantifiable information, the low likelihood that it is *reliable*). Many doctors are not trained to tell patients about all of the available treatment options, nor the pros and cons of different choices. Further, research also shows that health care professionals do not check to see if a patient has understood what they have explained.

And frankly, it's no wonder. Part of this is due to lack of knowledge; part of this is due to the pressures of the 15-minute office exam. And oftentimes there are numerous systemic pressures to make the patient fit.

As Oxford scholar and BMJ blogger, Dr. Richard Lehman writes, "Wherever we look in clinical practice, the evidence we have is often a poor match for the evidence we need. To conceal our ignorance and save us the trouble of dealing with uncertainty, we often behave like Procrustes when he invited guests to stay the night. If they were too short for his bed, he stretched them to fit: if they were too long, he cut a bit off them. One-size-fits-all treatment means that most of the prescribing we do e.g. for raised blood pressure, or for systolic heart failure, does very little good. We make the patients fit the evidence, shoving square pegs into round holes, especially if that earns us money. We need a different way of generating evidence and of practising medicine."

And we can substitute "health care system" for "evidence" in many of the statements above as well.

There is much more to say about this, why this is and more. And, therefore, some of you may be interested in reading our book that is written directly for patients.

> ## What You Don't Know Can Hurt You
> *A Guide for Patients*
>
> ### Help for Navigating Medical Information
> ### & Making Informed Decisions

Importantly, an effective evidence-based clinical quality improvement project can help close all of these gaps. In fact, an effective EBCQI project is oftentimes going to be the ONLY remedy for the pervasive systemic and chronic challenges in the health care universe that foil effective quality patient care and informative communications with patients. This is because an *effective* EBCQI project is information-centered and becomes systematized with gap-closing as its goal.

Patients *deserve* better.

A patient's journey to making a health care decision that is right for him or her can often be through difficult terrain, and **what you, as a health care professional don't know, can hurt patients**. Therefore, we want to **make you aware of some major problems** in health care *that you probably do not know about* and give you guidance to help you—as a clinical quality improver—to help clinicians and patients better navigate the health care universe.

We are *all* patients.

And when we say we are all about the patient—we are *all* patients—and so we are writing, too, about you.

And we want to help **you**.

So, having said this, let us now move into the 5 core requirements for EBCQI work and our outline for the 10 process steps that can help you efficiently and effectively achieve successful evidence-based clinical quality improvements.

THE 5 CORE REQUIREMENTS FOR EVIDENCE-BASED CLINICAL QUALITY IMPROVEMENT

A. Effective leadership demonstrably committed to an evidence-based approach, including providing support for the work;

B. A culture committed to high quality and patient-centered care and the appropriate use of evidence to achieve this;

C. A correct and effective evidence-based approach;

D. Correct work components which include resources, principles, concepts, structures, approaches, methods, processes, standards and tools; and,

E. Skilled and engaged individuals in the right roles.

THE 10 PROCESS STEPS FOR EVIDENCE-BASED CLINICAL QUALITY IMPROVEMENT PROJECTS

The 10 phases are—

Phase 1. Organizational Readiness

Phase 2. Clinical Improvement Project & Team Selection

Phase 3. Project Preparation & Outline

Phase 4. Evidence Identification, Selection & Review

Phase 5. Clinical Content Development

Phase 6. Impact Assessment

Phase 7. Communication Tools Development

Phase 8. Implementation—Create, Support and Sustain Change

Phase 9. Measure and Report

Phase 10. Update and Improve

While each of the phases is important, **Phase 4. Evidence Identification, Selection & Review**, is of paramount importance. At its heart, this book is about correcting some huge problems in the use and application of information and misinformation in health care decision-making, making important improvements in clinical practice and helping patients and care providers through you.

Consequently, your interest in this book is of vital importance in—

- Helping providers and patients know more about the quality of evidence for different choices;

- Making available choices for treatments that are more likely to have a better benefit/risk ratio;

- Reducing waste and missed care opportunities; and,

- Improving patients' abilities to have better and more patient-centered care—including making them better-equipped to make medical choices that are right for them and provide truly informed consent.

And, very importantly, you will be improving the professional knowledge of others who can go on to make further improvements for others, like a ripple stirring the ocean until it becomes a wave.

Think of this book as a guidebook, map and compass that can help you find the path to an efficient and effective evidence-based process for clinical improvement work and help you stay the course.

But first, we need to give you some background on what we refer to as the **"health care misinformation mess."**

Disturbing Facts: Does Any of This Surprise You?

1. You Need Reliable Medical Science + *Much* May Not Be Reliable

Physicians, patients, health care leaders—in fact, all of us—are making health care decisions every day. Good decisions require good information. And yet, every day patients are harmed and resources are wasted because they make decisions they would not have made if they had been better informed. An evidence-based approach to clinical improvement is required in order to reduce the use of unproven or unnecessary procedures and improve patient care.

You need reliable science to inform decisions about therapies. Yet, **most** published medical science—even in the most respected medical journals and by some of the most respected researchers or research institutions—is **not trustable**. Possibly up to 90 percent. We are not singling out industry-funded studies, either. Professor John Ioannidis "...charges that as much as 90 percent of the published medical information that doctors rely on is flawed" [Freedman]. One large review of 60,352 studies reported that only 7 percent passed criteria of high quality methods and clinical relevancy [McKibbon]. Fewer than 5 percent passed a validity screening for a highly respected evidence-based journal [Glasziou].

And such flaws mean that many interventions that are believed to be of proven benefit, in fact, may not be.

And you will not be saved by any source—not the Food and Drug Administration (FDA), not by utilizing only top-tier publications, not by rejecting all industry-sponsored science and not by relying on specialty society guidelines, which frequently are not based on sound science. And you should be wary of adopting recommendations from sources proclaiming to be "evidence-based," which is often misunderstood as simply citing references or the term is frequently used as a buzz-word. Even if you find a helpful source, you are still going to need some in-house knowledge of what constitutes reliability in medical science. (And if you are thinking to rely on your team members at your meetings, know that they are unlikely to possess these skills. And even if they did, they could only provide a little too late.)

2.   **You Cannot Solely Rely Upon the FDA**

Reliance upon the FDA is insufficient for medical decision-makers' sole source of information about the safety and efficacy of drugs and devices. The agency, for example, does not provide any information about comparative efficacy, safety or cost. Also, there are many instances in which reviewers may disagree that there is sufficient evidence of efficacy and safety.

3.   **It's Not "About Statistics" (Usually), But Issues Such as Study Design + Execution**

One of the first things we hear from people expressing a need to be able to evaluate medical science is that they need to know much more about statistics. However, some good news is that identifying studies likely to be unreliable is generally not about knowing more about complex statistics. Identifying study bias is key. (If you feel you need a statistical consult following that, find a biostatistician—but it should be rare that you ever need to do this.)

Bias is not about investigators personally favoring a treatment for some reason such as a conflict of interest—although that is important too. "Bias" means anything that leads away from truth other than chance. Studies have shown that **bias tends to distort study results by up to a relative 50 percent** or more [Chalmers,

Kjaergard, Lachin, Moher, Savovic, van Tulder]. Further, studies also show that bias tends to favor the intervention of interest.

A common result of not critically appraising studies before considering study results is that the evidence gets "upgraded," meaning that lower quality studies are judged to be of higher quality (i.e., at lower risk of bias) than they really are [Kjaergard, Reichenbach]. This, in turn, frequently results in the acceptance of results suggesting more benefit than actually exists or—worse— accepting study results reporting benefit when no benefit exists.

All researchers should be assumed to be biased in favor of what they are studying. Good study design and execution protects against personal bias affecting results.

More good news: The basics for evaluating studies for risk of bias are not that hard to learn. In fact, we are able to fit all of the key elements for basic core competency in evaluating the reliability of medical research studies on interventions on one 8 x 10 inch piece of paper.

4. When It Comes To Medical Science, Most Health Care Providers Are Operating In the Dark

Health care providers frequently do not know how **big the problem of unreliable medical science** is. Further, most of the physicians participating in your project only review abstracts. Abstracts are useful in that they can inform you about the relevancy of the study, and they can sometimes rule-out studies due to major design or methodological problems or through reporting results that are not clinically meaningful. But they cannot rule studies in as valid. Further, abstracts should be considered with great caution. One study found that 18 to 68 percent of abstracts in six top-tier medical journals contained information which was not verifiable in the body of the text [Pitkin].

5.   **Secondary Sources Cannot Solely Be Counted On To Help You + Many Cannot Be Counted Upon At All**

By secondary sources, we mean medical information sources that utilize primary and secondary studies—primary studies being the original research and secondary studies being studies of studies such as meta-analyses. Frequently secondary sources rely heavily on expert opinion and may contain low quality evidence. Examples of secondary sources include clinical guidelines, clinical recommendations, disease management protocols, compendia, health care economic studies, etc. Unfortunately, frequently the further one gets away from primary studies, the further quality seems to decrease.

Critical appraisal is a scientific evaluation of evidence (e.g., research data) to appraise validity (closeness to truth) and usefulness (e.g., generalizability to one's own patients or circumstances, meaningful benefit, etc.). Many secondary sources are flawed because often they do not include evidence that has been critically appraised and found to be reliable and clinically useful. This is true of many clinical practice guidelines—even from respected groups [Grilli].

As another example, when it comes to health care cost-effectiveness studies, it is rare that these studies employ an evidence-based approach [Jefferson, Stone]. Often the authors have not first established efficacy of an intervention through reliable evidence, which is the first necessary step to establishing effectiveness. Rather, frequently they build models on evidence that has not been critically appraised and may be centered on an intervention that, in fact, may not be beneficial at all.

6. When It Comes To Medical Science, Most Health Care Providers Are Operating Blindly

Worse, health care providers frequently **do not know *how* to detect unreliable medical science**. Health care providers frequently **do not know how to interpret study results**—even basic ones. Roughly, **over 70 percent** of physicians, clinical pharmacists and other health care professionals **fail** our simple 3-question critical appraisal training program pre-test [Delfini]. This is shocking. To give you a flavor of how serious this failure is, one question simply assesses the person's awareness of a need for a comparison group in an efficacy study. Without a comparison group, how would you know a condition wasn't self-limiting, for example, and recovery not due to an intervention?

Others have also reported health care professionals' lack of skills in assessing the quality of medical science, indicating insufficient training [Young]. For example, in one study of primary care residents, approximately 90 percent of the residents could not interpret 95% confidence intervals, statistical significance or the interpretation of Kaplan-Meier analyses; approximately half did not recognize the definition of bias (simple multiple choice question with 4 options); and, nearly 40 percent did not understand the meaning of a p-value of >0.05 [Windish].

But, good news again. We have found that health care professionals are quickly able to learn basic evidence-based medicine (EBM) and critical appraisal skills such as assessing studies for bias. Others have reported similar findings. For example, in one study, after only a few hours of critical appraisal training, residents and attending physicians increased their use of therapies proven to be beneficial in randomized controlled trials (RCTs) and, after the training, the percentage of high quality RCTs used as the basis for informing chosen therapies also increased [Straus].

7. Because Of All These Problems, People Die

Because of health care professionals' lack of understanding medical science basics, **people die who otherwise would not**. Let's look at some numbers from four examples. Importantly, each of these examples—out of many—were chosen because each represents a **failure to understand at least one simple basic concept which could have made a difference between life and death**.

Numbers below are estimates, but are likely to be either close or understated—

a) Over 63,000 people died from taking encainide or flecainide because many doctors thought this "made biological sense" [Delfini estimates based on Morganroth and Echt]. Ventricular premature contractions (VPCs) post-myocardial infarction were associated with a risk of sudden coronary death three times that of the men free of complex VPCs, and these agents were observed to be effective in reducing VPCs [Ruberman, Meinertz].

What was missed? What physicians did not seem to understand was the simple need for reliable clinical trial information to confirm what seemed to "make sense." With rare exception, only valid RCTs can prove cause and effect. (The rare exception is "all-or-none" results, meaning dramatic outcomes such as when the majority of people used to die before the application of a particular treatment which now cures nearly everyone.). Bonus points if you are concerned that physicians were relying upon an unproven surrogate marker.

b) An estimated 60,000 people in the United States died from rofecoxib despite important benefit and safety information that was reported in the abstract of a key trial [Graham] [Bombardier].

What was missed? Failure to correctly interpret study results, including an easy-to-understand statistic. Simple inability to differentiate (and be concerned about) a relative versus an absolute measure of outcomes. As it turned out, the FDA reviewed additional data, and it turned out that harms outweighed benefits. We spent years helping P&T committees not put rofecoxib on their formularies and discouraging physicians from prescribing it before it was pulled from the market in 2004.

c) Roughly 42,000 women with advanced breast cancer suffered excruciating side effects from use of high dose chemotherapy and autologous bone marrow transplant without any proof of benefit, many of them dying as a result, and at a cost of $3.4 billion dollars [Mello].

What was missed? Only valid RCTs can prove cause and effect, with rare exception.

d) At least 64 deaths out of 751 cases in nearly half the United States were linked to fungal meningitis thought to be caused by contaminated epidural steroids—but there is no reliable scientific evidence of benefit from that treatment, and the risk of serious adverse events has been well-established [CDC, Cohen, Iverson].

What was missed? The need for reliable science to inform medical decisions. **Patients cannot give informed consent** without being provided with reliable, quantifiable information on benefits and harms, and without being told about other potential impacts.

In each of the above instances, these were **preventable deaths and harms**—from common treatments—which patients might have avoided if **medical decision-makers** who play an important role in affecting peoples' choices—and lives—had better understood the importance of evaluating medical science.

Value can only be determined after information about the quality and usefulness of science is known. An evidence- and *value*-based approach to quality improvement **requires** a systematic review and synthesis of the evidence regarding benefits, harms and risks. Following that, other assessments can be made such as the trade-offs between other "triangulation" issues such as effectiveness, cost, alternatives, the patient's perspective, the organization's priorities, etc.

Critical appraisal is at the heart of evidence-based practice. It requires knowledge of critical appraisal concepts about what is required for reliable science along with clinical knowledge and critical thinking. In most instances, it is only by conducting critical appraisals of the medical literature for validity and usefulness that we can determine if an intervention is likely to be effective. And then there is the matter of safety. Safety information is usually quite limited, and months or years may pass before we truly know about safety and the net benefit of an intervention—if ever.

We cannot emphasize enough the failures we see as we travel around the country training physicians, clinical pharmacists and other health care professionals in the evaluation of medical evidence. We've worked with many health care systems and committees, we've assessed the knowledge of many seasoned professionals as well as faculty and recent graduates, we've had exposure to a lot of scientists—the story is largely the same. Concepts are not understood. Training is often poor—too little and/or too unnecessarily complex. Or application is poor—often made impossibly complicated.

Lack of awareness of these issues at the organizational level results in lack of appropriate criteria, methods, processes, skills, tools and support required to effectively and efficiently accomplish critical appraisal and other EBM tasks. This has resulted many times in poor outcomes for patients, health care professionals and companies, alike.

NOTES & DISCLAIMER

Use of this information implies agreement to our Notices at— http://www.delfini.org/index_Notices.htm.

Scope for This Book

At the book's opening, we described **What This Book Is About (And What It Is Not About...)** including that it is beyond the scope of this book to teach all aspects of clinical quality improvement or specifics about evaluating medical science. For this latter topic, we have a lot of information freely available on our website at www.delfini.org, and a book we have written on the basics of evaluating medical research studies.

Generally, our focus is on the **efficacy of therapeutic interventions**, unless we state otherwise.

We Give No Guarantees

Just as there are no guarantees in life, **we make no guarantees about this book** including accuracy of the information and whether it is sufficient and up-to-date. The information we provide to you, including on our website, is meant to augment rather than replace the clinical judgment of health care professionals or establish a standard of care. There are exceptions to everything we say. Often the most correct answer to any question we are trying to address is, "It depends."

Even Our "Fictions" Are Truthful

Some stories and cases we write about are true, but slightly altered to protect others' privacy or to better illustrate a point. Some are created from a variety of experiences or possibilities, and so are true in their potential, if not in their exact fact, to help illustrate our points.

We Will Repeat & Summarize

We find **we have to repeat a lot of this information to physicians, clinical pharmacists, nurses and others that we train**. For many readers, this information is new and may represent a new approach. Repetition can be an important method to help adults learn and change behaviors, and so you will find that we recomb, summarize and re-summarize key concepts at times.

References are in an alphabetized reference list at the end of this book. Authors are identified in text or sometimes are tagged in brackets [author name, year if multiple].

Resources include an **Appendix** at the end of the book, providing you with a sample critical appraisal, along with an address for a **Reader Resource** web page where you can find many additional resources that you can download. This will include a **glossary** and a **1-page critical appraisal checklist** that we always use when we evaluate the reliability of studies. This will also include **key outlines, lists and checklists** from the book so that you can download them, use them as checklists, adapt them into tools, etc.

A tool-based approach for performing clinical quality improvement work can prove extremely helpful for a number of reasons including helping you be complete and efficient. Because this is so important, we direct your attention to the **Reader Resource** web page **in each instance** in which there is a fit to content in the book. Therefore, you will see multiple references to a single tool or resource, for example, throughout the book. We do this so that you are reminded just-in-time in the discussion of each process step or consideration so you don't miss a related link to one of our external resources that may be of help to you.

In addition, a wealth of freely available and helpful resources can also be found at our website: http://www.delfini.org

Our Focus for This Book

We Are Writing For Patients' Lives + We Are All Patients; We All Need Reliable Science To Inform Our Medical Interventional Decisions

In this book, we place strong emphasis on the *reliability* of medical science. We cannot state this strongly enough: when considering the **benefits of therapies**—*only* with the rare exception of all-or-none results—observational studies (which includes most "real world data") are likely to give you the wrong answer. This includes your databases, no matter how large. Professor John Ioannidis has calculated that the positive predictive value of observational studies ranges from 20 percent to one-hundredth of a percent as compared to 85 percent based on valid RCTs [Ioannidis].

- We are *not* **saying** that you should never use observational data—it has value if used in the right ways.

- What we *are* **saying** is that, for **efficacy of interventions**, you need to start with reliable science and that means information from high quality (valid) randomized controlled trials (RCTs).

- Further, many interventions that are *believed* to have proof of efficacy, in fact, are **not supported by valid evidence**.

There is much more information on the appropriate use of "real world data" on our website www.delfini.org.

As we have stated, our books are dedicated to patients—and therefore to you and ourselves, as well. Our books are written because of the legions of patients who have been unnecessarily harmed due to not getting the right information. We write for patients who were unlikely to have been given information they needed for an informed choice. We write because of the incredible missed opportunities for right care and resulting waste from practices and decisions because of the lack of an appropriate evidence-based approach.

Let's talk about waste a bit because waste is a harm too. The estimates of waste in health care in the US (and very possibly many other countries), calculated by some very prestigious groups, are shockingly enormous at between 20 to 50 percent of all health care spending [Chassin, CMS, Kerr, McGlynn, Skinner]. If correct, these estimates mean that 20 to 50 percent of what has happened to each of us as a patient may have been a waste. We all pay for this in various ways including opportunity costs.

And so, we want to impress upon you—and you can contact us for more proofs than you find in this or our other books, if you need—if you want to help patients, improve care, save lives, not contribute to preventable deaths and harms or missed opportunities for care or waste—**for questions of cause and effect concerning therapies** (with the rare exception of all-or-none results, which we will expect you to remember at this point), you **_need_** to first obtain RCT information. You need to access RCT data, evaluate its reliability, make a judgment about its clinical usefulness and only carefully, knowingly and judiciously use supplementary information from observations. To repeat, your claims data and data from other large databases are observational. And you are likely to be misled if these data are not used carefully. Studies and examples show this again and again.

You need a truly sound evidence-based approach. Getting there may take you more resources, but you may make gains to support them if you do this work correctly. Learning how and what to do, however, is not that hard. You actually might save time if you have been expending a lot of effort doing the wrong work and/or in the wrong sequence. This book is about helping you achieve a truly evidence-based approach in an efficient manner.

You might also save money if the evidence does not support certain interventions. And so, an appropriate evidence-based approach might be financially worth an investment in resources overall, in addition to it being the right thing to do for patients.

Medical Science Boils Down to This

All this said, general questions about medical science boil down to these:

1) Are the **research results** likely to be true?

2) If yes, are they likely to be **useful**?

3) If yes, **to whom**?

4) If yes, at what "**price**?"

5) Are they "**usable**"—which has to do with issues such as, "Can you understand the results and act on them?" Thus, the importance of **trustable and useful medical science** is a key theme of this book— as is the fact that **much of the information you get is *not* based on reliable science**.

"Let's Start With The Evidence"

There is a plaque in Mike's office that reads, " *Mike Stuart, MD: The Father of Evidence-based Medicine at Group Health Cooperative— 1973 - 2002—'Let's start with the evidence.'"* The medical leadership at Group Health in Seattle, where we both worked for many years, was so used to hearing that phrase from Mike that they engraved it in metal on his retirement commemoration.

A family practice doc, Mike personally comes naturally to clinical quality improvement. In his own practice, he continuously sought ways to improve his own work flow, clinical and patient decision-making, communicating with patients and more. His work on his own personal projects caught the attention of the medical director who, in 1984, asked Mike to head up Group Health's continuing medical education (CME) department—to which he agreed. In his own words—

Mike's Story: Early Experience With Evidence-based Clinical Improvement—The Lipid Guru

In 1988, the National Cholesterol Education Program released screening and treatment recommendations [NCEP]. However, there was concern that the use of relative risk statistics could be misleading about absolute risk and risk reduction and benefit to patients facing decisions about whether to take a lipid-lowering drug or not.

Because of this, a few colleagues and I began a clinical improvement effort nicknamed, *The Lipid Guru Project*, to evaluate the benefits and risks of various lipid-lowering agents for patients with various risk factors. The project was sanctioned by leadership and administered through a collaboration between the Department of Medical Education (my department) and the Pharmacy and Therapeutics Committee. For this project, the group searched for, assessed and synthesized the evidence and created a guideline, successfully implemented it and assessed its impact, ultimately publishing the results [Stuart].

Having said this, I will acknowledge that none of us working on the project had a very good understanding about how to evaluate medical research studies for risk of distortion of results due to bias. That came later. But this was an important start, and our evidence review led to a very aggressive approach to non-pharmacological therapy and a very conservative approach to the use of lipid-lowering drugs in primary prevention of coronary artery disease.

Our goal was to educate clinicians at the local level by having one physician and one pharmacist function as evidence-based lipid experts and consultants in each of our 29 primary care clinics. Key elements of the program included—

1. A synthesis of the relevant medical literature;

2. Use of information systems including a laboratory computer that could calculate patients' lipid ratios and percentiles and print them on lab slips;

3. Algorithms, which, in clinical guideline work, are flow charts of a series of process steps for patient care, and other decision-support materials; and,

4. Feedback to clinicians and a core of "lipid guru" clinicians to administer the program at the primary clinic level following a one-day training session which included mini-lectures and case studies of representative patients who clinicians would be likely to encounter in the areas of primary and secondary prevention of coronary artery disease.

The project demonstrated that a formal, yet efficient, QI process for improving health care and decision-making was quite feasible. Staff satisfaction with the project was high (including primary care professionals, cardiologists and endocrinologists). The project also prevented overuse of lipid-lowering drugs. For example, in 1989, our lipid-lowering drugs cost 0.99 cents per enrollee compared to the national per-capita cost of $3.18. In 1990, our annual per-enrollee cost was $1.99 compared to the national per-capita cost of $4.22.

This project, and the subsequent "debut of evidence-based medicine" at our institution, led to our leadership's support of my request (and even providing some additional resources) to change a traditional CME department into one that also served as an evidence-based quality improvement department, using the medical education component as a conduit for implementation.

Why I Became Interested in Evidence-based Practice; And What I Did About It

When I speak of the "debut of EBM," my true understanding of what a true evidence-based approach meant came after the Lipid Guru Project. And so even though we reviewed and synthesized evidence for that project, I would have to characterize our work as "evidence light." Like the vast majority of physicians, I had only a very vague understanding of bias, how to identify it and the impact it can have on study results.

But early on in my career, even as a medical student and even for many years in my medical practice, I struggled with a feeling that I was never really getting reliable information. As a student, my instructors would offer differing explanations. As a practicing doc, I would phone up a couple of my colleagues in different specialties to consult with them—cardiologists, for example—and I would tell them about a patient I needed their help with. Often the advice I got varied, depending upon who I was talking to. I puzzled—and actually worried—over this. Was everyone right, and there were just different preferences they favored? Was one colleague right and the other wrong? (And then—a bigger worry—were they *all* wrong?)

When I was asked to direct medical education for our health care system, I knew I did not want to do medical education "as usual." In traditional medical education, frequently doctors just repeat what they were taught—sometimes many years ago—in medical school or at their specialty society meetings. Or talk about their opinions based on their "observations" and "experiences." But, frequently an opinion is just an opinion. And we have all been surprised, at times, by what we and others think we "observe" and "experience" versus what we later discover to be reality—and again, this holds true for doctors as well as for the rest of us. But I didn't know what to do to organize education programs for doctors and others that would center on trustable information that would lead to improved decisions.

Not, that is, until several years into my directorship—and in 1990 on the tails of our Lipid Guru Project—when, fortunately, a brilliant physician, Dr. David Eddy, began a series of articles published in the Journal of The American Medical Association (JAMA) on medical decision-making. The collection was ultimately produced in book form [Eddy 96]. In essence, David's key message was this: It's all about the quality of the science. And, unfortunately, most of the published medical science produced is not trustable.

This was startling to me because I had assumed—as do most practicing physicians—that I could trust my medical journals. I came to quickly learn, through looking at medical evidence in a new way, that I was wrong. Further, it was staggering to realize that there was a critically important deficiency in my medical training. What I discovered was that most of my colleagues and I were never taught how to correctly evaluate medical evidence to determine how sound it was or how useful it might be in helping patients.

This discovery was disturbing, to be sure. But this mattered for my patients, so I was determined to get on top of this problem, and when I am interested in something, I work hard to understand it. David Eddy's writings and my eventual personal conversations with him were like a super battery charge of my entire being. My enthusiasm and energy for medicine took an enormous leap. I loved the learning I was experiencing, and I felt a growing sense of gratification that I was going to be better at helping patients and providers in important ways. I got my hands on a variety of books and articles on research methods, epidemiology, statistics and decision-making and read and read and read—and did a lot of "hard thinking," as they say.

Evidence had a new meaning for me. I looked forward to every day of my new interest in learning and applying what I had learned to taking care of my patients and educating physicians. I did learn a great deal, and every day I give thanks to all those such as David and many colleagues and authors who have preceded me and helped me understand the role of critical appraisal of the medical literature—meaning the critical evaluation of medical research studies to understand reliability of results and more—and how to "package" health care information to be useful to patients and their care providers.

And, it was after my discovery of David, that I called my leaders and told them, "We need to change my department from a medical education department to an evidence-based machine!" To their great credit, they supported me even though this was a radically new idea. The Lipid Guru

Project was just the beginning. Over the years, our new EBM department produced numerous evidence-based clinical guidelines and pathways which we implemented at Group Health. And now, I'll let Sheri take over from here...

The "Evidence-Based Machine!"

What happened next was a combination of efforts from a number of dedicated patient-centered individuals, including both Mike and Dorothy Teeter, who later went on to work in leadership positions for various government entities including the Centers for Medicare and Medicaid Services and the State of Washington Health Care Authority. Motivated by Dorothy and several other leaders, a small collection of staff started an organizational-wide initiative to establish a series of patient-focused, population-based clinical quality improvement efforts, which included Mike's department. These efforts were centered around high impact topics such as primary prevention of coronary artery disease and diabetes—later adding additional areas to target. The goal was to improve clinical care processes and decrease unnecessary practice variation with the hope of improving patient health care outcomes, patient satisfaction and cost.

At the core of each of these clinical quality improvement efforts was a concerted effort to obtain the best information possible—with a focus on reliable scientific information. Mike established teams largely composed of clinical stakeholders supported with scientific and analytic help.

And we experienced some successes and great outcomes. Using the example of a single project—the dysuria project—which we will describe in greater detail later in the book, patient satisfaction improved and the organization saved an estimated half-million dollars per year.

Numerous clinical improvement projects were accomplished along with more than 30 evidence-based clinical practice guidelines and evidence-based pathways. By the time Mike left Group Health to form Delfini with me, he and his colleagues had helped not only our health care system, but others around the world, including the US Bureau of Medicine for the Navy and the Health Ministry of New Zealand. Numerous health systems were helped in their efforts to incorporate evidence-based processes and products, such as guidelines for doctors and other "evidence-based decision support" materials, into their work. This help came both in the form of guidelines and also in training and education on how to be an "evidence-based organization" and conduct evidence-based clinical quality improvement activities. Since then, as Delfini, we have helped others with various evidence-based quality improvement activities including not only clinical improvement teams, but also medical technology assessment teams, formulary management groups and others.

It's Not JUST About Science!

A key thing that we want to emphasize is that there can be *many reasons other* than scientific evidence for proceeding with a quality improvement or making a medical decision. For example, during our time at Group Health, administration approved the coverage of some treatments for rare conditions, despite lack of reliable efficacy information, for several reasons. In some cases, reliable studies were unlikely to be conducted. In one case, withholding coverage for a young mother who was insistent upon an unproven treatment could have landed us on the front page of the newspaper—and yes, there really is such a thing as bad publicity. (And, in any instances such as these, patients need to be informed of the lack of scientific evidence.)

So whether one actually starts with the evidence or another consideration— such as public relations issues, community standards, cost, liability, risk management, satisfaction of patients and clinicians or employers, etc.— is going to be unique to the particular context. That said, all too often decisions about medical interventions do not carefully examine the evidence. Therefore, our evidence-based clinical quality improvement work—and Mike's perpetual reminder to his bosses—**emphasizes science**.

We will say it again: reliable science leads to better decisions because of more **predictable** health care outcomes. Information about the quality of the science should be the right of all patients. Yet, the validity of science used to inform decision-making is frequently **misunderstood or ignored**.

What an Evidence-based Approach Is and What It Is Not

Let's start with what an evidence-based approach is not—and a final reminder here that there are exceptions to everything we say. In general, an evidence-based approach is **not** the use of a medical research study **without first evaluating the quality of the science** to determine **whether the results reported are likely to be reliable**. In short, this means that medical research studies need to be evaluated before they are used to try and ascertain whether the results are likely to be true or whether they have been distorted by bias. Again—and importantly, because this tends to be misunderstood—in the context of a formal evaluation of medical science, "bias" does not refer to the personal hopes of the investigators, but rather something in the course of the research that "leads away from truth" other than chance, such as lack of effective blinding.

Merely citing a study is not evidence-based practice. This is another common confusion we see. In the words of evidence-based medicine pioneer, David Eddy MD, listing one's favorite studies or simply referencing some citations is "evidence-sprinkling." And with all due respect to Dr. Eddy, even that term frequently may be too generous because evidence that is misleading is really not evidence at all.

In general, here are what we consider to be the hallmarks of, and ideals for, an evidence-based approach:

1. When seeking information on a topic, a **systematic search** is conducted for science and science-based information using evidence-based searching and filtering techniques.

At the **Reader Resource** page, we provide you with downloads to suggested resources for potentially reliable science, which may save you some time, along with some searching tools. Here are some things to know about systematic searching, in brief—

"Applying a systematic search" includes searching the National Library of Medicine, which is accessed through the online PubMed database. "Systematic search" also means that all relevant and potentially useful studies are sought, rather than studies being "cherry-picked."

Focusing solely on research about **efficacy of therapies**, evidence-based searching and filtering techniques would allow for **limiting studies** accessed to **randomized controlled trials** (RCTs) or systematic reviews of RCTs. We elaborate on potential limits and exclusions further in **Interview Questions to Help You Determine Evidence-Based Know-How and Sophistication**.

Searching for **safety** may be restricted to RCTs or may include observational studies. However, safety is still a cause and effect question and, therefore, the risk of misinformation is high. Remember what we shared with you about the positive predictive value for observations answering cause and effect questions [Ioannidis]. Example: Imagine that a new glaucoma medication has become available. You are monitoring your administrative claims data and see higher admission rates for patients using this agent. Did the agent cause the spike in admissions? Let us also say that a search of the medical literature reveals that high quality RCTs report that the agent has fewer pulmonary adverse events than the older drug used for the same indication. It is highly possible that clinicians are now prescribing the new drug to high-risk chronic obstructive pulmonary disease (COPD) patients, which explains the association between the new agent and the admissions documented by your database. This is an example of what is called "**confounding by indication**."

But because safety is often so difficult to assess and safety is so important, sometimes less reliable information is needed—but should be labeled with cautionary statements. The pyridoxine/doxylamine (formerly marketed in the US as Bendectin) story is a good example where an agent was no longer made available due to safety concerns, which were never proven—resulting in women being prescribed alternatives with a high risk of adverse events such as chlorpromazine (marketed in the US as Thorazine).

At the **Reader Resource** page, we provide you with an example of a safety review.

2. All sources of information to guide medical decision-making are **critically appraised**, using science-based principles, **for validity and usefulness**.

At the **Reader Resource** page, we provide you with various tools to help you accomplish this work efficiently. We also include an example of a critical appraisal there and another here in the book as well.

3. Methods used and reporting are **transparent** so that the work can be evaluated for quality and can be replicated and updated.

4. **Wording of any conclusions** drawn from the science is carefully crafted to be as valid as possible.

We provide you with a tool with sample language for crafting conclusions at the **Reader Resource** page.

5. Clinical information sources are **updated** when significant new information becomes available and such information is periodically sought.

EVIDENCE-BASED MEDICINE SKILLS + RESOURCES

Because the vast majority of health care decision-making professionals are **not** skilled in evaluating what constitutes reliable science, we are **not** going to assume that you are familiar with basic concepts, terms and principles. We are going to assume that this is all new to you. However, we remind you that it is **not** the scope of this book to educate on the totality of evidence-based practice and educate on critical appraisal. If you are a leader, we also know that many of you are not going to learn this—even though we think it is advisable that you do so for many reasons (including it is not that hard to acquire the basics and we, personally, feel it is important for your work). That said, we are writing this book assuming you do not have these basics, and we are going to try to help you navigate to create an evidence-based process without them.

For those of you who *do* want to learn the basics, there is a lot of helpful information online including a lot of information freely available on our website at www.delfini.org. We also have a short book available:

> BASICS FOR EVALUATING MEDICAL RESEARCH STUDIES:
> A Simplified Approach—And Why Your Patients Need You To Know This
>
> Delfini Group Evidence-based Practice Series

Because of the vital importance of critical appraisal and the reliance upon valid studies, at times we will detail some key critical appraisal concepts. At this juncture, we want to point out that there are two kinds of validity: **internal validity** which is closeness to truth in the context of the study and **external validity** which is closeness to truth outside the study (i.e., with other individual patients, populations or situations). **In this book, our focus is on internal validity**. Yours should be on both.

Evidence-based Medicine Resources

To give you the most up-to-date information we have, we will suggest some sources that may shorten your work for you at the **Reader Resource** web page. However, be forewarned that—

1. There is **no one source** that we can recommend to meet all of your evidence-based needs. You are going to need a variety of sources, in all likelihood.

2. Information contained in **any health care information source** we have come across may be of **varying quality**. Even sources you might assume to be "trustable" may have generally great methods, but other factors—such as politics, for example, or individual contributors' lack of skills—may affect the content in important ways at times that are not in keeping with evidence-based practice or which result in unreliable information.

Let's start with some terminology. Others may use different terms or use some of these terms differently. But here are our definitions:

Primary Study

The **original study research** in which direct measurements are made. Generally, original research is available through the National Library of Medicine (NLM). MEDLINE® is a bibliographic database of life sciences and biomedical information from the NLM. It contains journal citations and abstracts for biomedical literature from around the world and is accessible through PubMed® which provides links to full text articles when possible. Often, however, articles will only be available through purchase or subscription.

All primary studies must be critically appraised.

Secondary Study

Sometimes researchers perform a collective **analysis of multiple studies** together and report on their findings. Such an aggregate of results from primary studies is called a **secondary study** and ideally is undertaken in a formal way, which is called a "**systematic review**" (for example, a meta-analysis is a type of secondary study). If a review is not a "systematic review," then it is referred to as a narrative review or an overview. For questions of efficacy, the latter should only be used for non-evidentiary purposes such as gaining background information, understanding what is happening in typical practices or for safety signals.

All systematic reviews must be critically appraised.

Secondary Source

By **secondary sources** we mean **medical information sources that utilize primary and secondary studies**. These would include drug compendia, clinical guidelines, health care economic studies, protocols, etc.

(Guess what we are about to say...) **All secondary sources must be critically appraised**.

And so our very strong message is that any research study should be critically appraised for internal validity. You may choose to do this through your project team (and we provide you with a success story in which we efficiently reviewed all our primary studies in one collective group effort)—but they will likely need training and support in these efforts. You may choose to do this through (skilled) staff that provide information to the team or you may wish to find a source or content provider that does a good job of critical appraisal. In any instance, overall you need tips to help you evaluate whether scientific information about the efficacy and safety of an intervention is reliably evidence-based or not.

When finding outside materials or outsourcing, this includes assessing whether the source or content provider has and applies a solid evidence-based approach, including solid application of critical appraisal skills. You want to **obtain and review the criteria used to determine the validity** of the research relied upon. We emphasize this because there may be instances in which an author has good critical appraisal skills, but the criteria applied for the critical appraisal are poor. (And, in fact, we think this happens not infrequently.) We suggest that you compare any criteria to tools that we make available on the **Reader Resource** web page. You may also be helped through the questions that we will provide to you in the following section: **Skills**.

Beware the "**Book Report**." Oftentimes, we have seen output from those providing information content services that simply serves up an unexamined summary of the research. Critically appraised information should include a summary of the threats to validity which you can use not only for information, but also for a confirmatory audit.

In addition to seeking their criteria for a validity determination, if they use some kind of summary method such as a grading or tagging system, you should review their **criteria for the summation method** as well. There are many grading systems, some with similar labels or tags, and you should always review the criteria used as these may differ. Be aware that many grading systems are flawed which often results in the upgrading of poor quality evidence to receive higher marks than should be granted.

Another tip is that a high pass rate for RCTs is a strong indicator that critical appraisal is not being performed or is not being performed well. We and others who are experienced at this work find that we cannot pass as reliable evidence most of the studies we review.

Also, keep in mind that **clinical usefulness is generally a judgment**. If the information that you receive appears to be appropriately critically appraised, you may wish to start from scratch in considering clinical usefulness. Frequently, a determination of clinical usefulness is contextual. When considering the treatment of an individual patient, a physician may be more willing to judge as clinically useful smaller results (e.g., a smaller effect size) than a medical leader might when making a decision for population management purposes.

We want to remind you of the hallmarks of, and ideals for, an evidence-based approach. These are found in the above section, "**What an Evidence-based Approach Is and What It Is Not**."

Evidence-based Medicine Skills

No matter what resources you use, **you need someone on your project team, or staff to the team, who is truly skilled in critical appraisal of the medical literature** to be able to vet the resources, answer questions, evaluate information that comes through other sources, assist you in maintaining an evidence-based approach, etc. This could be a medical information scientist or other health care professional who has been effectively trained in critical appraisal—emphasis on *effectively*—and in our appendices, we try and help you determine that. Ideally, this person should have a key role in the project and should be seen as the subject matter expert on the quality of the evidence, having authority for establishing the final evidence grade, for example, and authority for other evidence-specific determinations. (From here on out, we will refer to individuals in these roles as evidence-based subject matter experts or EB experts.)

To provide you with the most useful guidance, we are going to give you advice which you can use to interview people—even if you lack these skills yourself—to increase the likelihood that you are getting reliable assistance. You will find this advice in **Appendix B: Interview Questions to Help You Determine Evidence-Based Know-How and Sophistication.**

However, identifying that person may be harder than you think.

Finding people with good critical appraisal skills is not a simple matter. It is vitally important that you understand the magnitude of this problem. We have trained thousands of people in critical appraisal methods. We've trained people immediately out of formal training in their schools as well as seasoned clinical professionals who have been in practice for many years. We've trained different kinds of professionals—physicians, clinical pharmacists, residents and students, nurses, quality improvement leaders, content providers, medical writers and more. We have trained people in different kinds of groups—government, payer, health system, content development, etc.—and we've trained people from all around the country. What we see is the same picture across all of these groups and health care cultures: most schools are not doing much by way of teaching students in health sciences about what constitutes reliable science. They generally do not teach practical approaches to the evaluation of validity and clinical usefulness of medical research—and many of those who attempt to do this training are not doing a very successful job or information is not used by those who are taught it and so is not retained.

The fact that very few people working in the health care professions who are involved in medical decision-making have a basic grasp of general critical appraisal concepts means that many interventional decisions are not supported by reliable science. Because some of you may find this illuminating, here are the questions and results of our critical appraisal pre-test.

Delfini Critical Appraisal Pre-Test

Question 1.

You read a report that 240 patients presenting with a number of symptoms are treated with Nuevo-Magico—a drug used for many years in Europe for various indications, and just approved by the FDA in the US. Symptoms are sometimes severe enough that people are confined to bed for a period of days. People may be ill for weeks. The disease is highly contagious and can be dangerous in the elderly. The side effects of Nuevo-Magico are documented in numerous well-done studies to be very rare—less than 1 percent have an allergic reaction, usually presenting as a mild rash. No long-term adverse effects have been reported over many years. Of the 240 patients treated, 232 patients are asymptomatic within 3-5 days of coming into the doctor's office. Because of a special program, there is no cost to patients.

Would this convince you that this agent would be appropriate for patients similar to those tested? If yes, why? If no, why not?

Remarks

Nearly 80 percent of physicians and 90 percent of clinical pharmacists tested failed this question because they do not notice the absence of a comparison group. (In fact, at one of the last places that we taught this, upon the "reveal," a physician cried out with some embarrassment, "Oh, no! And I suppose this is something self-limiting like a cold or the flu!" That is exactly right.)

Question 2.

A well done study reports a statistically significant relative risk reduction of 60 percent for patients in the intervention group, with a modest side effect profile. Would this convince you that this agent would be appropriate for patients similar to those tested? If yes, why? If no, why not?

Remarks

Over 70 percent of physicians we tested leap to yes. Clinical pharmacists fared better at a failure rate of nearly 60 percent. It was this amount of benefit that helped rofecoxib (previously marketed in the US as Vioxx®) become a blockbuster drug when the absolute benefit for preventing ulcer complications was less than 1 percent. So the relative risk reduction was 60 percent of less than 1 percent, thereby benefiting only one out of 125 patients in comparison to naproxen [Bombardier].

It is shocking how many physicians and clinical pharmacists have not been taught the difference between absolute and relative measures—especially when you consider how easy it is to calculate the absolute difference and how important it is to know as compared to the relative measures. (An absolute difference between groups is simple subtraction of outcomes in each group using percentages.)

What's more, many health care decision-makers focus on the absolute risk reduction (ARR) or the number–needed–to–treat (NNT), without realizing that these measures can mask meaningful information otherwise provided by the raw numbers of what happened to patients with and without treatment.

An ARR of 5 percent (the percentage difference in outcomes between the two study groups) may result in very different decisions if risk is high or low for an unfortunate event, for example. Imagine one scenario in which 95 percent of placebo patients experience an untoward event as compared to 90 percent of patients in the intervention group. Now contrast this with an inverse scenario in which 10 percent of placebo patients experience the unfortunate event compared to 5 percent of intervention patients. Consider: a patient who is risk averse and conservative about drug use might be less likely to choose an intervention when their risk of the untoward event is small, as in the second example. However, this patient might make the opposite choice if their risk of the untoward event is high, willing to throw risk of adverse events aside and take a chance that they might be one of the 5 percent who benefits in a lotto of otherwise unfortunate outcomes.

Question 3.

A study reports that 4.4 percent of 1629 patients are unavailable for their Intention-To-Treat analysis. No data were imputed. Comments?

Remarks
Failure rates for this question are high as many people have never heard of intention–to–treat analysis, and those who have heard of it usually misunderstand it. Intention–to–treat analysis requires that some outcome data be included for all patients randomized in the study and that patients be analyzed in the groups to which they are randomized. For dichotomous variables (meaning one of two choices, such as alive or dead), intention–to–treat analysis has been recommended to be the

primary analysis method for efficacy outcomes of superiority trials by editors of major journals.

Therefore, someone telling you that they know how to evaluate a study for reliability, that they received this training in school, that they studied epidemiology, that they went to Harvard or wherever, etc.—is not sufficient for you to feel confident that they have the needed skills. We have heard it all. And so we are going to give you some questions to ask. Before we do that, however, a couple of further cautions...

Beware the "Knowledge in a Microcosm" Seduction

So if we are correct and you are like most of the people working in health care decision-making that we have encountered, chances are very high that you lack critical appraisal skills including the ability to tell if someone else possesses them. That puts you at risk for being misled that you are getting truly evidence-based information or an employee or a vendor with reasonably sound evidence-based assessment skills.

If you, yourself, are not skilled at critical appraisal, and someone starts using terms that loom large (e.g., propensity scoring, regression analysis, biostatistical term-of-the-week, etc.) or they sound logical and in-the-know ("In this study, they didn't reach the number of subjects needed to be enrolled according to their power calculation for the primary outcome, so you should disregard it..."), you are likely to assume they have solid skills in critical appraisal—or at least know more than you know—and *you risk being wrong.* We are repeatedly amazed by how health care professionals have piecemeal knowledge—or mistaken "knowledge"—but no *core skills,* nor a *practical approach* for carrying out critical appraisal of medical information.

Beware the "Perfection Trap:" A Critical Appraisal Knowledge Reality Check

Critical appraisal is a process of discovery. There are some areas where controversy exists, and scientific understanding evolves. There are some areas where issues are popularly misunderstood, etc. So even those of us who are knowledgeable and experienced in critical appraisal can miss identifying a critical appraisal issue and sometimes struggle to find clear and helpful information. We are considered very knowledgeable in the area of critical appraisal and yet we are constantly learning. There is much that is unknown or that we don't know or that we may miss.

Therefore, you should strive to find knowledgeable people to help you in your mission of evidence-based decision-making. Yet, you should be realistic that ultimately, there is no "perfection" in this work—and so you should not expect it. Rather you should expect that everyone involved in doing critical appraisal has some gaps in their knowledge and is operating with some misunderstandings. Therefore, your expectations should be lowered as compared to what they might be for other types of knowledge—operating a vehicle, for example—but we can get you on the right road. And then it's largely a matter of doing the best one can. And we repeat—the best answer to many critical appraisal questions is, "It depends." So this work is frequently not a "one size fits all" situation.

After studying and teaching critical appraisal concepts and processes for many years—and having garnered some international respect for her work in this field—Sheri was invited to dinner by one of our most knowledgeable and respected evidology colleagues. As they toasted to each other's presence, eyes twinkling, he asked her, "So what's your understanding of the p-value?" She started laughing. "Are you kidding???" she asked. "No," he said, "I'm perfectly serious." Because he was clearly amused, Sheri thought this was the start of a joke—as it turns out it was, but the joke was on her. "It's the likelihood that you have chance findings," she said, still laughing, wondering what the catch was, having read much on the topic—including having been taught some key features about them by a leading biostatistician. "Well, actually," he said, with a knowing smirk, "it is not." This was *not* the punch line she was expecting. "But," he continued, still smirking, "everyone thinks that it is." And so Sheri began to unlearn and then relearn more about the very complex topic of p-values.

Our point of this story is that even those who are highly experienced in critical appraisal may be groping around in the dark at times. So, just as we describe validity as "closeness to truth," so too with critical appraisal. You want to get "close to proficiency" or involve others that are close to the mark. Happily, in most cases, this does not mean a deep understanding of statistics, but rather understanding the essentials of bias and the likelihood of chance effects. And happily, many of these concepts are based on logic—and so armed with a reasonable understanding of general critical appraisal concepts, by employing critical thinking coupled with some clinical knowledge, one can go far in discerning what information is likely to be reliable and clinically useful and what is not.

And, in case you were wondering about the "*true*" meaning of the p-value...

A Little P-Value Detour

After months of drafting and researching and redrafting, our "simplified" definition distills the issue down to this: "P-value - Assuming there truly is no difference between the groups studied (note that we are already on shaky ground because we start with an assumption), the p-value is a calculated probability of observing a difference as big as or bigger than the one you observed in a study based on compatibility with an assumed standard distribution."

How *complex* is the p-value that most of us thought so simple! How does one make graceful utility out of that?!??!? But to keep this detour short, the bottom line is that the p-value *cannot* tell you the chance that the results are due to chance. And therefore, the p-value has much more limited value than is frequently believed. Since what a p-value is actually about is somewhat byzantine and unhelpful, we tell people, "While the p-value cannot tell you the chance that the results are due to chance, it's an indicator of something like that..."

In other words, we are still using the p-value as an indicator that the results are due to chance—just with a bit more salt for uncertainty sprinkled into the mix. (But we should emphasize here that all these considerations about p-values are based on "reported" study results. It is meaningless unless you have first evaluated the study for bias and determine that the results are likely to be reliable.)

Bottom-line: Do not expect perfection in this work. There is (likely) none to be had. However, to increase your chances of getting good help, we will provide you with **Interview Questions to Help You Determine Evidence-Based Know-How and Sophistication** in the **Appendices**.

EVIDENCE-BASED CLINICAL QUALITY IMPROVEMENT = 5 CORE COMPONENTS + 10 PROCESS STEPS

A review and a transition. Again, ideally, closing gaps through EBCQI projects requires several **core components**. These are—

A. Effective leadership demonstrably committed to an evidence-based approach, including providing support for the work;

B. A culture committed to high quality and patient-centered care and the appropriate use of evidence to achieve this;

C. A correct and effective evidence-based approach;

D. Correct work components which include resources, principles, concepts, structures, approaches, methods, processes, standards and tools; and,

E. Skilled and engaged individuals in the right roles.

A reminder that our 10 EBCQI phases are (which will we review in detail in upcoming sections)—

Phase 1. Organizational Readiness

Phase 2. Clinical Improvement Project & Team Selection

Phase 3. Project Preparation & Outline

Phase 4. Evidence Identification, Selection & Review

Phase 5. Clinical Content Development

Phase 6. Impact Assessment

Phase 7. Communication Tools Development

Phase 8. Implementation—Create, Support and Sustain Change

Phase 9. Measure and Report

Phase 10. Update and Improve

Phases 4, 5 and 6 are largely the impetus for the decisions for what happens to patients. Yet, all too often clinical "improvements" are not evidence-based. Often they bypass the evidence review part of **Phase 4. Evidence Identification, Selection & Review**, going directly from gathering evidence to **Phase 5. Clinical Content Development** by adopting a clinical practice guideline or some other outside resource such as a clinical recommendation or disease management protocol—**without critically appraising it—and ensuring it is updated with critically appraised information**. Before we get into the details of the phases, let us take a little detour, going deeper into **Should You** with a specific focus on clinical guidelines, as an example.

A BIT ABOUT CLINICAL PRACTICE GUIDELINES

A lot of clinical quality improvement teams often start out with adoption or adaptation of a clinical guideline. So it is important for us to talk a little bit about clinical guidelines and provide some deeper cautions.

Clinical guidelines have been developed for many decades in an attempt to systematically gather and present information to assist decision-makers, but—among other problems—frequently they do not include reliable critically appraised information, they may not be transparent, and they may not include detailed implementation strategies found in good EBCQI projects.

The Institute of Medicine has described what it considers to be the requirements for high quality guidelines. In broad strokes, guidelines must be developed through a transparent process which combines critically appraised evidence, expert opinion based on clinical experience and a consideration of patients' preferences and values. The IOM considers these eight standards essential to developing sound practice guidelines [IOM 2011]:

1. Establishing transparency;

2. Management of conflict of interest;

3. Guideline development group composition;

4. Clinical practice guideline–systematic review intersection;

5. Establishing evidence foundations for and rating strength of recommendations;

6. Articulation of recommendations;

7. External review; and,

8. Updating.

Well-done evidence-based clinical guidelines can improve care and optimize use of resources. But unfortunately many guidelines vary greatly in quality.

For example, Kung et al. found, in an analysis of a random sample of clinical practice guidelines archived on the National Guideline Clearinghouse (NGC) website as of June 2011, very poor compliance with IOM standards, with little if any improvement over the past 2 decades. The overall median number (percentage) of IOM standards satisfied (out of 18) was 8 (44.4 percent). And, as many guidelines used by clinical improvement teams come from subspecialty societies, it should be of extra concern that barely a third of the guidelines produced by these groups satisfied more than 50 percent of the IOM standards surveyed.

Information on conflicts of interest (COIs) was given in fewer than half of the guidelines surveyed. Of those guidelines including such information, COIs were present in over two-thirds of committee chairpersons (71.4 percent) and 90.5 percent of co-chairpersons.

Except for US government agency-produced guidelines, criteria used to select committee members and the selection process were rarely described. Committees developing guidelines rarely included an information scientist or a patient or patient representative. Non-English literature, unpublished data, and/or abstracts were rarely considered in developing guidelines; differences of opinion among committee members generally were not aired in guidelines; and, benefits of recommendations were enumerated more often than potential harms. Guidelines published from 2006 through 2011 varied little with regard to average number of IOM standards satisfied [Kung]. (Note: Although we are reporting all of these as research findings, we urge caution about a couple of these items. Including a patient on a clinical improvement team should be done very thoughtfully—and we will give you our advice for this soon. Further, some of the data sources mentioned here—e.g., abstracts—are likely to be of uncertain validity.)

Another important issue not addressed in the Kung review is the paucity of critically appraised information. We have seen numerous examples of guidelines published by professional societies which are based on weak or fatally flawed evidence such as in the areas of cholesterol screening in children and interventions for spinal pain.

Others have reported similar findings. For example, Giannakakis et al reported that, although the use of RCTs in developing clinical guidelines has increased, almost half of the guidelines appearing in journals such as the Annals of Internal Medicine, BMJ, JAMA, NEJM, Lancet and Pediatrics do not cite RCTs [Giannakakis].

Grilli et al., in a review of 431 guidelines produced by U.S. medical societies, found that—

e) 87 percent did not report whether a systematic search of the literature was performed;

f) 82 percent did not apply explicit criteria to grade their evidence; and,

g) 67 percent did not describe the type of professionals involved in the development of the guideline [Grilli].

The issue of low quality clinical guidelines is partly due to a **fairly universal lack of effective training for the health professions in understanding scientific validity**.

We recommend that users of guidelines and other clinical recommendations scrutinize all such documents for validity and usefulness rather than relying on endorsement by professional societies, reliance upon which, in some instances, may lead to suboptimal outcomes.

At a minimum, we suggest the pertinent questions are these:

1. Are the recommendations **rigorously evidence-based** and their development **transparent**? This requires understanding principles of scientific validity and should include your performing a critical appraisal, or at least a critical appraisal audit, of the science upon which the recommendations are based. There are many resources available to help readers evaluate information sources for validity. Readers need to know the strength of the evidence associated with each recommendation.

2. Is this information **relevant** to patients' needs? Are the expected outcomes clinically significant and will they provide reasonable estimates of benefit? Are the important recommendations/options (with benefits, risks, harms, uncertainties, alternatives and costs of each choice) provided? Do the recommendations accommodate differing patient values and preferences?

3. Can this quality improvement be **implemented** and is it likely to succeed? How will the guideline impact outcomes in the setting in which it is applied? Can one measure the effect of implementation?

4. How **current** is the information?

5. **Who developed** the recommendations? Were epidemiologic and clinical perspectives included? Were other disciplines and perspectives represented as needed?

6. Are any **limitations** described?

7. Are there **ethical** issues to be considered

Although guideline peer-review is desirable, we believe that the type of checklist above provides a more appropriate solution for the evaluation of clinical guidelines for validity and clinical usefulness than specialty society development and endorsement because it helps remove the bias which may be present in any group making clinical recommendations based on consensus and low quality evidence.

In conclusion, we believe that any group including **any information from clinical guidelines or other secondary sources should evaluate those sources for validity and clinical usefulness** before accepting any recommendations from the secondary source, no matter how prestigiously-sounding the group. Several groups (including ourselves) have created tools to evaluate clinical practice guidelines—which also can be used to help structure your own or create adaptations. A link to our evaluation tool is available at the **Reader Resource** web page.

That said, let's get down to the steps...

DETAILS ON THE 10 PROCESS STEPS FOR EVIDENCE-BASED CLINICAL QUALITY IMPROVEMENT

To proceed with an evidence-based project, requires the **5 EBCQI Core Components** (1. support, knowledge and effectiveness through leadership; 2. committed culture to evidence-based patient-centered care; 3. true evidence-based approach; 4. correct and supportive work components; and, 5. skilled, engaged individuals in needed roles) + **The 10 Process Steps For EBCQI.** Many of the details we discuss below are reproduced, in condensed format, at the **Reader Resource** web page for downloading.

IMPORTANT: A linear format requires that we present information in a linear fashion. Our 10-phase process is actually a fairly accurate description for an effective and efficient sequence for process steps for EBCQI work. However, these steps should be thought of more as dance steps than as steps up a flight of stairs to reach your destination. At times, the steps require a bit of flexibility and suppleness, and so you may need to move through them in a more fluid way. (*Dance* your way up the stairs!) Plus, what we are describing below represents an ideal, and sometimes not all the steps are taken or are necessary. So think of this as a "guide," just as a clinical practice guideline is not a standard, but only guidance.

Phase 1. Organizational Readiness

Your first phase is about ensuring that you have the core components that are needed for performing effective EBCQI work. Later will come ensuring that you have all the components you need for your specific project which we will discuss in **Phase 2. Clinical Improvement Project & Team Selection**.

A. Organizational Leadership

Let us start with the organization itself: Is commitment to an evidence- and value-based approach demonstrated in written documents of core values for the organization such as in the mission statement, in a value or quality plan and/or business plan? Effective EBCQI can occur without these; however, an organization that is truly committed to evidence-based clinical quality improvement will reflect this by formal expressions.

What generally *is* required is a commitment **by leadership** to an appropriate evidence-based approach. This includes either direct and effective support or willingness to express support as needed. This also includes the provision of resources including time.

Further, organization commitment is also reflected through formal operational structures. Effective EBCQI can still happen without the equivalent of an evidence-based quality improvement department, for example. But the right organizational structures in support of an evidence-based approach can help float or sink the appropriate use of evidence, can help an evidence-based culture thrive and can help the organization survive the loss, through turnover, of individuals who are standard bearers and champions of evidence and skilled at evidence-based work.

And so, what if you are lower down on the totem pole and are wishing to propose a clinical improvement project and your leaders are not "leading with evidence in mind?" What might you do about this?

Firstly, we have only rarely seen a champion for an evidence-based **process** emerge from top leadership. We think this is largely a product of lack of awareness and absence of effective evidence-based education in the health sciences, health care administration, and so on. Often, the recommendation for taking an **evidence-based approach** comes from a unique individual—a "champion"—but for EBM, in this instance, as compared to a project.

Either instance can be a good thing. In the instance of commitment to an evidence-based process arising from leadership—provided they follow through with the other components—life is good! If, however, the recommendation for an evidence-based process comes from someone farther down the food-chain, it usually requires educating leadership on why an evidence-based process is vitally important to patient care and to reducing waste. We have provided you with some important facts you can share in this book, and we will also provide key information you can use at the **Reader Resource** web page.

In short, if your leaders are not leading in the context of *evidence-based* clinical quality improvement, educate them! Tell them stories. You need them to be not only on-board, but to be proponents and drivers. They set priorities. They provide resources. They can motivate and set tone. They can create structures and infrastructures.

Ultimately, leaders must understand and utilize the methods of an evidence- and value-based approach in order to effectively improve outcomes. **Leaders must teach, encourage, demonstrate and persuade as well as establish norms, incentives and systems that place "value" at the center and root out inadvertent "penalties" for taking the net view.** As an example, budget silos may compromise a department—and, therefore, jeopardize a clinical improvement's successful implementation—when a shift from a surgical approach to a medical therapy approach occurs.

You need your leaders. We have seen highly committed individuals go it alone—but then, all too often, what happens is that the unsupported individual becomes a short-timer or burns out, they leaves or abandons the effort and there is no one to carry the evidence-based quality improvement banner. Ideally, if you are emerging from the rank and file, you will get multiple leaders committed and on-board. We have **frequently watched good evidence-based work die** because it was dependent upon an individual or a few from the rank and file without it being institutionalized. Your efforts for any project that helps patients are worthwhile—but isn't it best if you can create a lasting legacy?

B. Culture

For an evidence-based culture, the principles, concepts, approaches, methods, processes, standards, tools—and importantly skills—of EBM must thrive in the committees, work groups and daily lives of health care professionals. Leaders can help affect the culture as can other formal and informal leaders.

Cultural elements that can foster success or contribute to the failure of an EBCQI effort include—

- Formal and informal **leaders**;

- Understanding and **commitment** of the culture generally;

- **Attention** to opportunities, improvements, hazards and sustaining what works;

- **Learning** environment; and,

- **Adaptability**.

And sometimes cultural issues present a big challenge. We advised you to tell stories; now we are going to "talk story," as they say in Hawaii, to you.

So in talking about culture, one happy cultural event for us was that we were hired to facilitate several clinical improvement projects in, of all wonderful places, Hawaii! However, Hawaii also has some very unique features culturally which can be a bit challenging at times.

One of the projects we were hired to help with was a clinical improvement in the prevention of venous vein thrombosis in total hip and total knee replacement surgery (hereinafter referred to as the **VTE project**) with Kaiser Permanente Hawaii. We won't go into all of the challenges, but several conspired to make communications tough—which was one of the reasons for the project.

One problem is that in the Hawaiian island community culture, if you are polite, one doesn't "talk stink" as they say—you don't say anything bad about anybody. So there is a cultural imperative that can get in the way of open communications if something isn't going well. And this can be further exacerbated by the fact that there are some very distinct lines that people may be discouraged from crossing, and these can run along both status and, at times, gender lines, which can also hamper open communications and acceptance. And while these communication issues can be found operating on the mainland US, in Hawaii sometimes these can be magnified and take on some special flavors.

Another issue is that problems arose because of differing points of view between surgical, medical, hospital and pharmacy specialties. According to the leadership, there had been a gridlock for so long that people just stopped talking about VTE prophylaxis because of the discomfort associated with these discussions.

So a key point is that your EBM leaders need to be facile at identifying key features of your own local culture and try and understand what may help or hinder evidence-based quality improvement work.

In the project leader's words, "A frank approach helps in addressing underlying reasons for not participating and solving those issues." And this enabled her to get people to participate in the project.

But then importantly—after people agreed to be involved—some with tremendous reluctance—it was the medical evidence that turned the course of things. Evidence tends to be a neutralizing force when all team members understand what makes for a valid and clinically useful study—and this is another reason why taking an evidence-based approach is so important. An evidence-based approach helps move away from opinion, which is frequently charged with emotion—and opinion, is frequently only as good as a guess. We've seen tremendous change for the good when people move toward a consideration of the evidence—in a truly evidence-based way.

C. Evidence-Based Approach

We discussed earlier **What an Evidence-based Approach Is and What It Is Not** . In the upcoming, **Phase 4. Evidence Identification, Selection & Review**, we will detail, in greater depth, more about what an evidence-based approach actually is.

D. Correct Work Components: **High Level**—Many Specifics to Follow in Upcoming Sections

These include—

a) **Principles & Concepts**

Those engaged in evidence-based practice need to have, at a minimum, a general understanding of evidence-based principles and critical appraisal concepts. The deeper you can go, the better! As we have shared with you, we are able to fit all of the key elements for basic core competency in evaluating the reliability of medical research studies on one standard-sized piece of paper (readable without microscope). Ensure that people are trained, at least in the basics.

b) **Approaches, methods, processes and standards (which needs to include updating)**

We will provide you with much guidance and advice for what you need to accomplish in the upcoming, **Phase 4. Evidence Identification, Selection & Review**, as well as providing you with many resources at the **Reader Resource** web page.

c) **Information and access to information**

"Resources" means a number of things, but includes information and access to information as a part of work components. At the **Reader Resource** web page, we will give you our best suggestions for evidence-based information resources that are more likely to give you a higher yield of reliable information. However, even with these sources, you should apply some caution as all the sources we have reviewed have variability in terms of reliability (i.e., information passing a rigorous critical appraisal). Your best remedy is to have rigorous critical appraisal skills yourself or on hand. Access is a bit trickier. As we've mentioned, a lot of this information is only available through purchase or through a subscription.

d) **Tools**

You may find other tools that you prefer, but we will give you a big selection at the **Reader Resource** web page. We have an even greater wealth of freely available information at our main website at http://www.delfini.org.

e) **Considerations and decision mechanisms**

We will provide you with an **EBM Committee Deliberations Tool** at the **Reader Resource** web page.

f) Communication aids and mechanisms (internal, external)

This means communication mechanisms in several contexts. This includes the development of clinical communication aids (information, decision and action aids) resulting from the project and to be discussed in **Phase 7. Communication Tools Development.**

This also means communication mechanisms you need up and down the line involving leadership, EBCQI team members and stakeholders including patients and providers, along with anyone engaged in other needed activities such as implementation, measurement, reporting and updating.

g) Implementation mechanisms

Upcoming in **Phase 8. Implementation—Create, Support and Sustain Change**

h) Measurement mechanisms

Upcoming in **Phase 9. Measure and Report**

i) Feedback mechanisms

Upcoming in **Phase 9. Measure and Report**

j) Resources and time...

E. Skilled Individuals in Needed Roles

And nothing can happen without the right individuals with the right skills in the right roles. This includes skilled and effective managers, project leaders, workers and work groups. We will elaborate more on what's needed in the upcoming section.

Phase 2. Clinical Improvement Project & Team Selection, Plus Meeting Management Tips

In this section, we address several things important for setting forth on creating clinical improvements: selecting a project and selecting a project team along with identifying project leadership, which we save for last.

Project, project team and project leadership decisions have no linear order, in general. Rather, the order for making these decisions is a result of **unique contextual factors.**

For example, a formal leader may mandate a project and may or may not be involved individually. An individual from the ranks might identify a project of interest that he or she wishes to champion or may propose a project, but not end up leading the project. A project might surface via a formal committee or because of some contextual need. A department formally charged with clinical improvement may be hunting out project opportunities. Project leadership may precede the establishing of a team, or leadership may be determined after the team is identified.

However, because of the interrelatedness of the project, who works on it and who leads that work, we think it is useful to address each of these three decisions in a collective section. Therefore, the information in these sections should not be thought of as linear in progress at all—but rather should be taken in a more piece-meal or stand-alone fashion, allowing you to apply as befits your individual context.

We include bonus tips: Success of a project—and whether project operations go smoothly—can be helped by effective preparation and processes. Therefore, we will also include in this section some **meeting planning and management tips** for EBCQI projects.

THE EVIDENCE-BASED CLINICAL QUALITY IMPROVEMENT PROJECT: SELECTING GOOD PROJECTS

There is a saying that "**evidence is global, clinical quality improvement is local**." While this isn't true one hundred percent of the time, it's roughly true. When it comes to assessing the efficacy and safety of health care interventions, you may make a serious mistake in interpretation if you rely upon your local information, such as queries from your administrative databases. Rather, you want to rely upon reliable and clinically useful evidence obtained from high quality medical research studies.

When it comes to clinical quality improvement, the application of this evidence in a systemized way in your organization is dependent upon **local factors** such as your five core components: leadership, culture, approach to evidence, work components and individuals. Therefore, you need to look at localized factors to answer such questions as what are our needs, can we meet them, how, is it worth our effort, can we measure our changes, what's the best way to report them, and so forth?

In most cases, EBCQI projects should be initiated only after carefully considering whether the effort is likely to pay off in terms of improved health care outcomes, patient or clinician satisfaction, cost/utilization or other important considerations such as liability issues. A useful way of thinking about what EBCQI projects should do is to consider the concept of gaps. There may be a gap in the current quality of care as compared to optimal care or when new evidence becomes available. You may be facing problems with underuse, overuse or misuse. There may be a knowledge gap. For example, clinicians may benefit from knowing the current state of the evidence regarding benefits versus risks of various therapeutic options.

These and upcoming considerations are available as downloadable templates and checklists at the **Reader Resource** web page.

Key questions include—

- Is there a **closable gap** between current care and optimal care (e.g., in health care outcomes, satisfaction, cost, etc.)?

- Do we have an important area of **medical uncertainty** that can be diminished?

- Do we have important and inappropriate **variation** in practice that is not explained by patient need or choice?

- Are there opportunities for change which provide **advantages** over current care?

In general, the **size of the gaps** and **likelihood of closing those gaps** should be the major factor in considering how many resources will be devoted to the EBCQI project, assuming it is more than a minor undertaking.

Once a candidate for a project is identified, some key considerations for deciding to proceed or not include—

1. **Importance** of area for clinical improvement;

2. Useful and usable **evidence** upon which the quality improvement can be based;

3. **Stability**—what's the likelihood of future change, obsolescence, etc; and,

4. **Feasibility**—organizational ability to carry out the improvement; and,

5. **Measurability** of the quality improvement.

Importance and Patient Health Care Outcomes

If the gap is about improving patient outcomes, keep in mind clinical significance (clinical outcomes that matter to patients) versus intermediate markers (i.e., outcomes that are "assumed" to stand in as proxy for a clinical outcome e.g., tumor shrinkage not known to improve patients' survival or quality of life) *unless* there is solid proof that the intermediate markers truly result in a beneficial clinical outcome. The clinical outcomes are these five and size of benefit is an accompanying consideration—

1. **Morbidity**;

2. **Mortality**;

3. **Symptom** relief;

4. **Functioning** (e.g., mental, emotional, physical); and,

5. Health-related **quality of life**.

For improving patient health care outcomes, you want sufficient, useful and usable evidence to draw conclusions regarding cause and effect relationships between clinical interventions or care processes and health care outcomes.

Evidence Considerations

Useful and usable evidence is—

1. **Valid**;

2. Likely to result in net **clinical benefit** (i.e., areas of clinical significance and size of efficacy and safety outcomes);

3. **Relevant** to the population, is applicable and considers the patient perspective;

4. **Acceptable** to physicians and patients including benefit/risk ratio, unknown factors about the intervention, etc., (e.g., if the technology is new without good evidence or if the evidence base is small, issues may include the learning curve for physician competency in use of

the intervention, unknown likelihood of patient adherence and more); and,

5. **Actionable** (ease of use or application of the intervention).

If there is not likely to be valid and useful scientific evidence—if this is for a health care outcome—our recommendation is do not do an "improvement project." It may not be an improvement at all, but more of the same (and yet costly and time consuming to achieve through a project that doesn't really improve anything) or it may actually create harm or waste.

Feasibility

You want to choose a clinical improvement that is achievable. Even if you have core organizational components institutionalized, there may be gaps for a selected project. Once you have identified topic candidates, a first step in assessing organizational readiness for a specific project may be to think of that project as a microcosm and re-review the 5 core components and 10 EBCQI process steps contextually.

For example, you might have a culture committed to an evidence-based approach, but something about this particular topic is uncomfortably controversial, making acceptance or progress especially challenging. Or you have skilled people in critical appraisal, but the topic—maybe infectious disease or use of biosimilars—is sufficiently complex or unknowable for your organization that you aren't likely to be able to be very clear about the quality of the evidence.

At this stage, it is important to contemplate possibilities for project leadership even if assignment of leadership will come following the identification of the team. In most cases, an EBCQI project cannot easily move forward without a "champion." A champion is an individual—usually a clinician—who has all the desirable attributes of a good project leader for the specific type of project to be conducted, and thus, frequently will become a leader within, or the leader of, the workgroup.

If you are the person who has proposed this project, are you ready, willing and able to invest the time and the energy needed to serve as project leader? Are you capable and willing to lead the team? Can you commit to updating? If not, are you aware of someone else who can take on these roles or assist you in them?

Or, if you are an organizational leader who is mandating this activity top-down, you want to ensure that you have a capable, enthusiastic, effective and committed individual or individuals who can lead the project. Leadership considerations are listed just after we discuss identification and assembly of the EBCQI team.

You are likely to do various feasibility assessments or check-ins along the way. The two most key may be your preliminary one and an especially key one, after obtaining needed information and before deciding to actually implement the project, which is addressed in **Phase 6. Assessing Impacts of Practice Change**. In addition to the factors we have just mentioned, your **preliminary feasibility** assessment should take into account a host of considerations including—

1. What is likely to **change**? Think of this in a detailed way. Here are some **considerations**:

    Health, cost, clinical practice outcomes, patient satisfaction, physician satisfaction, systems, utilization & administrative impacts (facilities, systems, roles & skills), methods (including procedures, equipment, supplies) and other resources, along with capacity, and any other issues such as those listed in our triangulation issues list below (which is taken from another source and so repeats a few of these items above) .

    > **Triangulation issues**: accreditation issues, community standards, cost, customer/employer issues, ethical considerations, liability and risk management issues, marketing, media or press issues, medical community

impacts, medical-legal, public relations, purchasing issues, regulatory, research realities (e.g., likelihood that no evidence will be available to answer clinical questions, harms of new technologies are frequently not known early on, etc.), utilization (e.g., impacts of provider change including demand, whether you have the capacity to support this change, impact of substitution, etc.) and overall impact on your organization.

2. Will changes in clinical care be **achievable, measurable and acceptable**?

3. Is **implementation** of the quality improvement feasible?

4. Are organizational **structures, systems and processes** in place for supporting change? This includes maintaining the change. This also includes tracking and monitoring ability and feedback mechanisms.

5. Will **leadership** support the change?

6. Will the **culture** accept the change?

7. Are **resources** available to support the initiative including time?

8. What are the incentives, barriers and disincentives? Can **driving and restraining forces** be understood and addressed?

9. Is an **internal champion** for the project available? (More on this to come when we discuss project leadership.)

10. What are **timing or timeline** considerations?

Source Ideas for Possible Project Content

Here are some ideas for resources you might research to identify ideas for projects. Reminder that **all sources** used to inform **medical interventions** must be evaluated for reliability (validity).

1. Clinical practice guidelines;

2. Systematic reviews (meta-analyses are a type of systematic review) or other research studies;

3. Clinical algorithms;

4. Clinical compendia and other sources making recommendations;

5. Clinical quality improvement projects;

6. Pathways;

7. Protocols;

8. Disease management strategies;

9. Utilization management strategies;

10. Benchmarks;

11. Accreditation targets;

12. Consensus statements, etc.

Additional Project Selection Tips

1. Toggle back and forth between **internal and external information** to find gaps. For example, in one of our guideline projects we became aware of the lack of evidence supporting clinic visits and laboratory studies before treating otherwise healthy women for "bladder infections." We toggled between the published evidence on the

problem and our organizational data and found that we were supporting overuse of visits, urinalyses and urine cultures. We determined there were efficiency, quality and satisfaction gaps and proceeded to create a guideline allowing low risk women to simply obtain antibiotics after a standardized phone interview.

2. Focus on **fixable problems**.

3. Along with your feasibility considerations, create a preliminary "**balance sheet**" to try and anticipate impacts of practice change (see balance sheets in **Phase 6. Assess Impacts of Practice Change**). This includes not only cost, but other impacts of change as well. This exercise performed early can help with your value assessment to decide if this project is worth going ahead with.

4. Start with a project that is not too complex and **likely to succeed**— you will evolve faster with early success.

THE EBCQI TEAM

The kind of organization that you are, the kind of customers you serve, your purpose, etc., should all be considered when determining your criteria for membership. Selection of team members should also be based on qualities of leadership, experience, skills, enthusiasm, effectiveness and worker-qualities (such as seeing a task through to completion efficiently and effectively, diligence to understand system issues, taking personal responsibility, being self-motivated, is a good team-member, etc.). We have already shared with you that your pool for selection is unlikely to give you very many choices of health care professionals who have much knowledge of evidence-based practice, so you will **need to account for this**.

We cannot stress enough that **you need an evidence-based subject matter expert** to lead your team on, at least, the evidence-based tasks. You have some choices about team leadership, tasking and decision-making—but our advice is to ensure that your EB expert is seen as having some leadership and decision-making authority as part of their formal team charge. You are more likely to have a truly evidence-based outcome as a result than if they are just considered staff to the project.

If do not give your EB expert a more formal leadership role—say co-leader along with a clinical lead—then you **must take care that the project team leader assumes the role of the champion *for the evidence***, looking to the expertise of the evidence-based expert for help and guidance. Otherwise, evidence-reliability has a good chance of derailing.

Your team should be constructed with an understanding of how various tasks will be accomplished such as critical appraisal of the medical literature and obtaining general information such as disease incidence overall and local information such as disease incidence in your population or current practice, cost data, etc. Will staff be available to perform some or all of these functions? Or will tasks be divided among team members to complete as they are able? (Shortly we will share you our great story of how we got an entire team engaged in critical appraisal, producing evidence reviews in record time.)

For most organizations, the selection of members, importantly, will involve **key stakeholders—ideally key opinion leaders**—who will become core team members and who will consider the evidence and expert opinions expressed at meetings. This will be of vital importance as the team will reach conclusions; create recommendations; and, develop implementation, communication, measurement and reporting plans—some of which may be controversial. And, because evidence-based clinical improvement and guideline projects *can* be controversial, the choice of invited opinion leaders should consider (carefully) those who may be a hindrance to a project as well as those who may be helpful to it.

The selection of team members and/or staff involves a consideration of **key task bearers**—such as leaders, project managers, evidence-based subject matter experts, analysts and/or librarians—who can do such tasks as obtain evidence, other key information and internal organizational data for the group.

Although representation most typically on EBCQI projects comprises health care professionals, sometimes other groups such as patients are represented. We would advise carefully thinking through consumer membership. Ideally, the consumer/patient representative has some experience with the business or the provision of health care. Otherwise, in our experience, the lay member frequently is really only able to represent a narrow set of perspectives. If the team does include a patient representative, we suggest selecting an individual with more health care knowledge and experience than a patient working outside the health care field. Or someone who has experience representing a variety of patients.

No matter the specialty area of the topic, we generally encourage including representation from primary care physicians. They are often affected by clinical improvement projects either up- or down-stream or are involved in advising patients.

This would be sufficient reason alone; however, there is another important reason as well. Primary care physicians tend to be especially open and receptive to evidence-based practice in comparison to other specialties. They tend to be willing to learn evidence-based principles and apply them. In meeting proceedings, when they have evidence-based knowledge, they often end up serving as the standard bearers of an evidence-based approach to decision-making. However, they usually **have to be encouraged to speak up**. Inform them that this is part of their role.

Ten is a nice number for a project team, even twelve. Having worked with many work groups, we have discerned that the team functions best when the number of core team participants is less than 15. More than that tends to become unwieldy and more challenging for people to be able to actively participate during meetings.

Ideally, all of your members are enthusiastic, hard-working and committed, and ideally they are interested in being good "citizens" on your team. But clarity and expectation setting is always good and so...

Get Agreements Up Front

Prior to acceptance as a project team member, ideally invitees are provided with a project letter of understanding or something in writing that documents their agreement to important key items in advance. (When we have failed to follow our own advice, we have paid for it—believe us!) These may include the following—

1. Your statement of the project **purpose**;

2. Their specific **role** including your expectations for who or what they represent;

3. Your general expectations for members including **disclosures** of conflicts of interest; agreement to become and remain **knowledgeable about basic critical appraisal concepts and methods**; review **materials** prior to the meeting; and, agreement to **meeting norms** such as responsibility to come to meetings prepared to discuss the issues, acceptance of your lead evidence-based subject matter expert's clarifying evidence issues when an opinion clashes with the evidence, timely start, completing assignments, etc.

4. Your general expectations for members' participation in **project tasks**;

5. Your **rights of terminating** them from the project for any reason at your discretion;

6. Your **commitment to evidence-based practice** along with an expression of **what this means**—

Example

"We value the use of valid and clinically relevant information to help inform medical decision-making. Many studies in the published literature, in fact, are at high risk of bias, uncertain risk of bias or at high risk of chance effects. Our project membership includes an evidence-based subject matter expert who is tasked with making final decisions about the quality of the medical science we may use to inform our project. Many physicians, nurses, clinical pharmacists and other health care professionals involved in medical decision-making have not received much training in understanding risk of bias and chance effects in studies. If you agree to participate in our project and, if this is true of you, we will provide you with opportunities to understand more about risk of bias and chance effects in studies. As a project member, you agree to apply generally accepted critical appraisal concepts in discussions and decision-making."

7. General **logistics** such as meeting frequency and location.

Tasks, Skills, Training & Orientation

EBCQI teams require effective leadership, training and support along with the right skills.

Tasks & Skill

Special skills, support or facilitation needs include those which can result in accomplishing these tasks—

1. Construct a **clinical question**;

2. **Search** and **filter** the medical literature;

3. Identify needs for, obtain and analyze needed **internal and external data**;

4. Develop a project **focus statement**;

5. **Critically appraise** and grade the medical literature;

6. Create **evidence syntheses** (i.e., evidence summary statements with quality of evidence tags);

7. Create **clinical recommendations** (including tags for the strength of the recommendations);

8. Assess potential **impacts of practice changes** and create balance sheets;

9. Formulate **guidelines**;

10. Generate **tools for practice** such as algorithm, 1-pager, protocol, risk stratification tools, formulary information, diagnostic aids, etc.;

11. Develop or identify appropriate **communication aids** such as information, communication and action aids for patients and providers;

12. Create and execute plans for **implementation**, **measurement** and **reporting**, including feedback planning;

13. Accomplish necessary **updating**; and ,

14. Accomplish necessary **documentation**.

Training

All *EB*CQI project team members (note the stress on "evidence-based") should have **basic proficiency in critical appraisal of the medical literature**. The likelihood they need training in these skills is high. Ideally, they receive no less than a day of effective and condensed training in critical appraisal (in our experience, ideally 2 days of training—the addition of this time is exponentially better for the gains…) or some effective substitute for that, unless they already have proficiency in this area. (If you think they do, consider that **this is rare** and take care in determining that this is actually true.) You will not only be helping the project processes and decisions, you will be giving these members a gift—and one that keeps on giving to them professionally and to their patients—and to them when they are patients as well.

In our experience, training sessions for clinical quality improvement members that provide the participants with an understanding of evidence-based medicine and the important elements of critical appraisal considerations provide tremendous payoffs in terms of the efficiency of project team meetings and the quality of the decisions that are made, as well as often eliminating controversies (and the impact of their attending emotions).

Even when members are proficient in critical appraisal, we strongly urge their participation in any such training session that you might have on this topic.

Generally people who are experienced in evidence-based practice have become that way because of interest. Even when we provide the most basic critical appraisal training, our most enthusiastic participants are frequently those who have the greatest evidence-based medicine knowledge. When we have such experienced people in our training seminars, we comment openly that we appreciate having people participate as co-trainers with us in an informal way. Having them participate in the training enriches the training experience for other members and signals that they are leaders in this knowledge area and helps to put everyone on the same page with respect to evidence, including approaches, terminology, etc.

Another important benefit of this training can help the success of the project at later stages. For example, the communications about decisions and the implementation of change can be eased if all project members can be engaged as informed **evidence-based** opinion leaders to help educate colleagues in their own select cultures. Understanding an evidence-based process and key elements of critical appraisal can help this because your project members can educate and help further an informed focus on the evidence, the benefits for patients and more as well as use evidence to help smooth out conflicts due to "valuing" low quality evidence or opinion that runs counter to quality evidence.

Further—and importantly—you may be seeding an evidence-based culture. Our clinical improvement projects with Kaiser Permanente Hawaii were actually born from a goal to move beyond organizational training in evidence-based methods and actualize and apply the training, developing a cadre of seasoned evidence-based clinical improvement practitioners along the way.

Orientation

In addition to ensuring their understanding of the essentials of critical appraisal along with other EBCQI activities, orientation and training should ideally be in person or at least voice-to-voice. Orientation should include the following—

1. A review of **their agreement** to your memorandum of understanding as outlined, at a minimum, in **Get Agreements Up Front** above;

2. If considered advisable, a review of your **definition of conflicts of interest**—and which might include a requirement that they sign a conflict of interest statement;

3. A review and **discussion of evidence-based practice**;

4. An explanation of **project decision-making and implications of decisions**;

5. Orientation to any **standard project materials**; and,

6. A reminder of **logistical** information.

Physicians generally end up being the most looked to for project team decisions. Often, non-physician members feel uncomfortable speaking up in the presence of physicians. For these members, orientation should include a specific recognition of this and provide encouragement that they speak up.

And don't assume this applies only to members who are not physicians. Primary care physicians—especially if not internal medicine—are often quieter especially when another specialist is present during a discussion in the specialist' area of expertise. They need to be encouraged to speak up too if they perceive an evidence-based approach is being overlooked.

Team members need to understand their roles in EBCQI activities. They frequently need to be oriented to effective participation by understanding how they should prepare for each meeting, what is expected of them in terms of meeting norms and the consequences of their decisions. Going a bit deeper, we believe they need to—

1. Understand the importance of the team in **protecting patients** from adverse events and improving their lives;

2. Understand the team's **aims, standards, criteria, methods, processes and tools**;

3. Understand the vital **importance of critical appraisal** and what that means;

4. Know the basics of **how to effectively critically appraise** primary studies, secondary studies and secondary sources of health care information;

5. Distinguish between **observations and experiments** and understand what all-or-none results are (and how rare);

6. Determine when "evidence" is not **valid** evidence;

7. Appreciate that, with basic skills in critical appraisal of the medical literature, he or she can play an **important role** in health care issues involving specialties other than his or her own;

8. Commit to **ongoing learning** about how to effectively evaluate medical evidence;

9. Understand the **problems of surrogate outcome measures**;

10. Know the 5 outcome areas of importance to patients—the **clinical outcomes** being morbidity; mortality; symptom relief; emotional, physical and psychological functioning; and, health-related quality of life;

11. Be able to quickly discern the difference between **opinion and evidence**;

12. Be effective at making determinations by **triangulating evidence** with other important factors such as patient preference, regulatory issues, cost, etc.;

13. Come to meetings **prepared** to discuss agenda items and participate in decision-making to the best of his or her ability; and,

14. Be **proactive and vocal** in project issues when he or she sees an important study flaw or other problem such as the need to remove a drug from the formulary.

Some of these elements are included in a 1-pager on **Being an Effective Evidence-based Committee Member** available at the **Reader Resource** web page, which you can add to as needed.

EBCQI PROJECT LEADERSHIP

At the outset of this phase, we discussed how decisions about project leadership will be based on your unique contextual factors, plus choices are many and may include both vertical and horizontal layers. We gave some examples of some of these variations.

Most typically, there are projects that are led by champions (usually clinicians) or projects that are led by assigned project leads (often not clinicians). There are also projects that are led by team leadership (clinical/administrative dyads or multiple leaders with specific areas of decision-making authority, responsibilities or skills).

Using the VTE project as an example, we had several kinds of leaders, in fact. We had top organizational leadership, we had a structural leader, we had clinical leads and evidence-based subject-matter leaders who were expert in EBCQI processes and science.

To break this down, the project was sponsored by Grant Okawa MD, who was medical director leadership—so we had formal support from the very top of the organization. Authority and management for the project on a daily basis were vested in EBM structural leader, Karen Ching MD. So Karen's leadership was structural and practical, and importantly, it was motivational as well as she was the voice of Kaiser Hawaii for the group. We had two project physician co-leaders from two of the main clinical stakeholder groups. These physicians were the key clinical decision-makers. We had pharmacy leadership as well. Delfini principals (we two authors) were EBM experts, guideline development and EBCQI process leaders and overall project facilitators. In these latter roles—and partly because of the time-limitations of others—we were the chief project movers, shakers and worker bees, with others making the internal organizational processes flow. A lot of leaders to create our little village, but it worked beautifully because everyone knew what they were leading and had the necessary skills.

In thinking of assigned leadership for your project, important considerations include what support do you have at the top of your organization (especially who is the holder of resources); what will it take to get the job done and who can best make that happen (this may be more than one individual—be clear about roles as we were); and, what obstacles need to be removed and who is most likely to be able to accomplish this?

Importantly, does the project have a "champion?" And since usually this will be a clinician, from here on out, assume that our use of the term "champion" means "clinical champion," although that won't always be the case.

If there is a project champion, typically this is great news. However, generally a clinical champion will need some kind of co-leader or key team-mate who can help accomplish leadership, system, process and other tasks. Conversely, a non-clinical assigned project leader will typically need a co-leader clinician identified to participate for clinical knowledge and getting buy-in and support.

A key difference in flavors could be characterized in the following ways—

- Clinical Champion-Leadership Driven: Frequently, mission-driven to make change due to personal experience and subject-matter expertise; probably less savvy about things like meeting leadership, needed documentation, etc. Often, benefits by having day-to-day administrative leader involvement.

- Assigned Leader: Often this is going to be a person who is not as close to the clinical question, but is a structural or administrative lead who is directed to make change due to an organizationally recognized need. This person is probably more savvy about process, management, leading meetings and less knowledgeable about clinical issues. The *assigned* leader needs to create an atmosphere and environment that makes up for what having a champion lacks. Therefore, this leader usually needs committed clinical participation at a leadership level.

In thinking about your leadership, consider ideal leader qualities, roles, responsibilities, needs, etc. which may require a combined leadership approach—

Ideal Leader Qualities

1. Recognized and accepted as a **respected** leader (or good potential to be);

2. **Enthusiasm** and **commitment** for the work;

3. **Willingness** to perform all needed aspects of the work;

4. **Interest** in and good **knowledge** of the topic (willing to adjust after understanding reliable evidence, if not known before);

5. **System savvy** and possesses insight into **local considerations** that relate to the project, including cross-specialty, -professional and -departmental lines, varying layers, silos, etc.;

6. **Communicates, motivates** and **works well** with project participants, stakeholders and others who may affect or be affected by project processes and outcomes;

7. Ability to **contract** with team members, inspire them to work hard and be skilled at **conflict prevention and resolution**;

8. **Persuasive** with organizational leaders for needed resources;

9. Possesses **effective meeting, project and process management** skills;

10. Good **manager of effecting change**;

11. **Works hard** to do what is needed;

12. Willing to serve as an **ambassador** for the activity; and,

13. Willing to continue to **support and update** the project, when new information becomes available, for example, and assess the project's impacts.

Leader Roles and Responsibilities

1. Understand each step of the EBCQI process and anticipate next steps;

2. Obtain necessary support from leaders as needed;

3. Form work teams;

4. Ensure the establishment and organization of meetings and manage them;

5. Inform other members of the organization regarding work progress;

6. Assist with reminders of various logistics;

7. Lead and/or participate in major steps such as critical appraisal, evidence table creation and evidence synthesis;

8. Trouble-shoot and problem-solve as needed;

9. Assure completion of work documentation;

10. Lead work on final products;

11. Obtain approvals as needed;

12. Implement the practice change;

13. Be an ambassador for the work, representing the work for the good of the organization and the good of patients; and,

14. Stay abreast of the measurement outcomes and any emerging valid and useful evidence, updating as needed.

In general, you need some type of leadership, support and/or facilitation to make these things happen.

Some Meeting Management Tips

What we are about to describe might sound to you like it is really more in the realm of **Phase 4. Evidence Identification, Selection & Review**, and some subsequent stages, but it really is not. It really is about **process steps and some ideas for efficiencies** and will help you better think about how to best identify your leaders and construct your team, as well as how the work might be accomplished. Phase 4. is more about how to actually *do* an evidence review; this is more about tips and efficiencies to *getting it done*.

We are going to share with you, in a general way, how we accomplished training and the completion of a clinical guideline in record time using our VTE project example. More granular details are available at the **Reader Resource** web page.

Before We Begin; Quick Backgrounder

Necessity is the mother of invention, as they say. We (Delfini) had little support, and so we were on the hook for much of the project work for the VTE project and needed to be smart and creative to keep from getting killed from task overload.

Before We Began

Often running an effective meeting requires more work outside of the meeting than during. Project and meeting management tools were vital for us.

The entire membership and others with whom we needed to routinely communicate was put into a word-processing document table. This made it easy to record attendance, and the email column could just be copied and pasted into an email to send the minutes out.

We did the minutes ourselves. Having experts do minutes just-in-time means they can be very short, be accurate and omit unnecessary information. We saved time by not having to review a support staff person's attempts and try to wrestle with fixing that.

Minutes did not just record what went on during the meeting, but were project records as well. As an example, our standard project phases were put into the document and completed as we went. Project scope, agreements, key findings—anything like that went into the minutes template. So each time minutes were distributed, members, leaders and others had all the key information in their most recent document. No one needed to hunt to find out key information about where we had been, where we were at the moment or where we were going (in so far as we knew).

In the minutes, we always made assignment lists with clarity about who was to do what task and by when—each and every meeting. And this was a topic item for each and every following meeting.

It was also important for us to **prepare the *meeting* in advance**—to do this, **we created the *minutes* "in advance"** to the extent we could, including thinking up assignments and next steps.

The minutes were then actually "finalized" just-in-time during the meeting, reviewing key items with members verbally at the meeting's end. We scheduled 30 minutes post-meeting to get them done and get them distributed immediately using our aforementioned word-processing document table.

Critical Appraisal by Committee

In **Phase 4. Evidence Identification, Selection & Review**, we will focus on critical appraisal. Right now, we want to discuss some meeting management processes that helped us complete the VTE guideline in record time.

In Sheri's words—

We knew that getting through the critical appraisal work was going to be the biggest hurdle. Almost none of the team members knew how to critically appraise a study. Not much support and about 50 trials to review meant we (meaning Mike and I) had to get clever (or be buried).

We did much of the planning work by phone, but we decided we needed two 2-day in-person meetings: one 2-day set for critical appraisal training and actually doing critical appraisals; and, the other 2-day set for coming to agreement on creating the clinical recommendations (after synthesizing the evidence in between through email and phone meetings) and preparing for next steps, plus training and planning for the subsequent EBCQI project phases.

Training on the core concepts of critical appraisal was highly condensed (one half-day) and then largely just-in-time via the critical appraisal activities themselves (a day and a half). And we were in Hawaii! That gave us the idea for the "open air" office!

We got a great big room, and we put a large table to seat 4 to 5 in each of the corners. At each table was a clinical expert—in this case an orthopedic surgeon or a hospitalist—and at each table was also a pharmacist and an EBM expert, such as Mike, Karen or myself. And then other team members were sprinkled around.

Prior to the event, I created critical appraisal capture templates. For this project, we knew we needed to just capture essentials. If a study was rejected by a group, they could just write that—along with the reason for rejection— on a study copy. However, the rule was that if a table chose to include a study, they needed to complete the critical appraisal form for that study on their PC.

The word processing template was developed to record not only the critical appraisal findings, but also to capture project documentation and—

importantly—capture key information if we were going to utilize the study to get everything we could just-in-time to move us to the next level. Elements included—

1. Study identification information;

2. Team information documentation;

3. Potential threats to validity;

4. A qualified assessment of outcomes (e.g., safety);

5. Study grade;

6. If the study was to be included in the guideline—

   a. Results to be utilized;

   b. Key study details as desired (we will talk about **PICOTS** more later, but this consists of patient, intervention, comparator, outcome, timing and setting), adding an additional "P" to the mix (**PICPOTS**), standing for "performance outcomes" such as adherence outcomes or special contextual elements of the care experienced by study subjects);

   c. Key author conclusions, along with key reviewer (meaning our team) conclusions; and,

   d. Anything else needed for ultimate subsequent tasks including evidence synthesis, clinical content development, impact assessment, communication tools, implementation, measuring, reporting and updating.

A sample template is available at the **Reader Resource** web page. A columnar format allows for cutting and pasting to be able to view information about multiple studies collectively.

Each table had a computer with someone to do the typing. Again, importantly, this was not a support staff person, but someone expert from the team.

Judiciously (thanks to the wisdom of one of the clinical leads), it was also someone other than Mike or me—i.e., *other* than an EB expert. Because of our size as a team with limited EBM expertise, Mike and I still had a primary table assignment to ensure that we had some EBM expertise for each group. But we also were "*the*" EB experts for the entire group. And so, being freed from recording information enabled Mike and me to be both participants at our tables, but also free-floating, as need be. As the project facilitators, EBM experts and process leaders, this was important to let us interact with others at other tables, just-in-time, but still guide the evidence reviews at our own tables.

The critical training being so condensed and, since critical appraisal was new to most people on our team with the exception of Karen and a few others, our first reviews were more like group exercises. We had copies made for each team member of the first several studies so that we could do the first appraisals collectively as a group and do just-in-time teaching as need be until Mike and I felt confident we could let the tables operate with greater independence.

This didn't take long and, once we were satisfied we could 1-2-3 go, we told members that this was going to be a competition to get through the rest of the critical appraisals.

Following the first couple of studies that we appraised as an entire group, we put enough copies of the remaining studies for a single table in a cross-hatched stack in the center of the room. At this point, each table would be responsible for an individual study appraisal. The minute a table finished appraising their study, they would go to the stack and grab copies for their table of the next study. This way we moved through the stack of the 48 remaining studies with the greatest efficiency, having no down time at the tables which would likely have occurred if we had divided up the studies equally among tables.

Announced meeting norms included that anyone could ask for help from anyone else in the room or a table could call for a consult with the whole group. Again, Mike and I were the prime movers for anything non-clinical in the physician and pharmacist worlds and so helped with any EBM questions and adjudicated process decisions as needed.

We also had online confidence interval calculators at-the-ready which we used a lot. Upon better understanding how to use them to interpret clinical significance and how easily they could calculate them, confidence intervals became very important to the clinical leads. For example, in the safety sections of the total hip and knee replacement trials, bleeding rates in the study groups were frequently presented without p-values or confidence intervals. Bleeding is of great concern to orthopedists because it delays hospital discharge and complicates joint rehabilitation after surgery. Hence, the need for confidence intervals to see the range of possible differences in bleeding rates when drug A was being compared to drug B.

The group reviewed the completed templates in a meeting over the phone or email. Then Mike accomplished **Phase 4. Evidence Identification, Selection & Review > Evidence Synthesis and Summarize the Evidence** with the clinical leaders over the phone, and we placed key information about selected studies into an evidence table. Then, at the second 2-day in-person session, we reviewed the evidence tables and, as a group, we constructed the clinical recommendations—meaning **Phase 5. Clinical Content Development**.

And again, that meeting also included training on subsequent EBCQI steps such as implementation and decision-support which they would be doing on their own.

Important Advice for Project Leaders: We have described to you that frequently we have seen the problem of evidence being mixed up with opinions and falsely labeled, "evidence." Project leadership (including EB expertise) must be able to discern when this happens and must skillfully manage the evidence review followed by a discussion of other considerations. It is important that the team lead not allow opinion to override evidence; rather, opinion should be used to fill evidence gaps. Again, ideally the lead or other individuals on the project are extremely knowledgeable and competent in the area of critical appraisal of the medical literature to clarify what is evidence and what is opinion.

Phase 3. Project Preparation & Outline

This is the phase for getting "prepared for the work." In this phase, you are developing out what the project is going to be and how it will be accomplished. This may include steps such as establishing timelines and milestones, selecting or creating process steps and tools, etc. For example, in this phase, you may do activities such as—

1. Create a **focus statement** for each project and subproject and draft your **clinical questions**;

2. **Draft an algorithm** and/or a template which will evolve as evidence is reviewed (more on this to come, and this may involve use of a "seed" secondary source such as a clinical practice guideline);

3. Determine potential **sources to use to find a foundation for the project, such as a clinical practice guideline, and/or other sources for information**;

4. From the **10 Process Steps for EBCQI**, determine which **process steps** you are likely to use;

5. Obtain **agreements** from leaders, team members and others, as needed, in key areas such as processes, timelines and milestones;

6. Establish **mechanisms and processes** in preparation for **Phase 4. Evidence Identification, Selection & Review** such as those needed for compiling background information, identifying potential evidence sources, drafting a search and filtering strategy, selecting tools for reviewing the evidence, etc.;

7. Decide upon **grades and tags** for quality of evidence and strength of recommendations; and,

8. Develop **documentation** plans and tools.

You also may need to **reassess resources** and review and clarify **roles** at various points as you make discoveries during your preparations, including ensuring you have the needed **skills, resources and allotted time** available to perform the work.

Details and tools for some of these tasks, such as **searching and recommended sources**, are available for download at the **Reader Resource** web page. Here are a few details pertinent to **clinical questions** and your preliminary **algorithm** draft.

Focus Statement & Clinical Questions

Whether doing a systematic review, clinical guideline or evidence-based CQI project, a good starting place is the set of **key clinical questions** which will serve as the compass for the project. **The aim of the project is to answer the questions and convert the answers into communication aids, such as decision support materials, for others**.

Key questions in EBCQI projects usually deal with questions about comparative effectiveness, safety and costs. Frequently, the questions require discussions between experts in the clinical area and stakeholders and, at times, require preliminary literature searches to estimate the availability of potentially useful evidence.

Project outline is all about project focus and scope. Especially if you are new to EBCQI work, start with a project that is not too complex and likely to succeed—you will evolve faster with success. Break down large projects into "bite-sized" segments. Mantra: smaller the scope, the greater likelihood of effective accomplishment.

Let's assume that your starting point is your clinical question. Constructing the clinical question will drive the scope and shape of your project and the resulting information. For example, the question, "Do the benefits of this therapy outweigh the risks?" will result in a very different kind of review than the question, "How does this therapy improve treatment, safety and value for patients with a given disease compared to other treatment options?" Be clear about your focus and be clear about your scope.

The following key clinical questions were developed by our VTE prophylaxis team and used for the project outline:

1. What is the evidence that thromboembolism or deep vein thrombosis (DVT) prophylaxis with various agents reduces mortality and clinically significant morbidity in hip and knee replacement surgery?

2. What is the evidence regarding timing of anticoagulant prophylaxis for appropriate agents when used for prevention of thromboembolism in hip and knee replacement surgery?

    •   What is the evidence regarding starting anticoagulant prophylaxis?

    •   What is the evidence regarding duration of anticoagulant prophylaxis?

3. What is the evidence regarding bleeding from thromboembolism prophylaxis with the various appropriate agents?

We will return to constructing clinical questions in **Phase 4. Evidence Identification, Selection & Review > 2. Identify Potentially Useful Evidence** because you will refine your questions in preparation for your evidence search.

The Straw Man Algorithm

Before our work on the VTE project, we also worked with KPHI on a chronic kidney disease guideline. As we were being transported to the Hawaii airport by our nephrologist colleague with whom we had been working, Mike pulled out a pen and a napkin he found in his pocket. "Okay, Brian," he said to our driver, "if you had to make up the ideal guideline—without knowing anything about the evidence at this point—what would it look like?"

At Group Health, Mike ensured that we had created algorithms or flow charts as part of the decision support for a clinical practice guideline. The algorithm was essentially the guideline, in succinct mapped-out format, on one single piece of paper. (We always joke and say that docs like 1-pagers even if the text is so small you can't see it—just get it all on 1-page! And, in fact, in our experience, this has pretty much turned out to be true.)

I peered over into the back seat, watching as Mike started drawing squares, arrows and circles. "Are you serious?" I asked him. "Depending upon what we find, isn't that just going to be a wasted effort?"

"No, not at all," he said. "It gives us a structure, even if wrong. We just replace as we become informed by the evidence and delete what doesn't fit." And so, roadway rolling on before us with palms waving overhead, the two doctors started making up an algorithm and completed their task just as we arrived at the Honolulu International Airport, about to be whisked away into the world of flight-fun and napkin-contemplating.

In fact, it turned out that this was a brilliant strategy—and we've used it ever since when developing clinical practice guidelines. Creating a "straw man" guideline/algorithm was like having a map to help us know what boxes we needed to fill. It kept us organized and on track. It gave everyone a one-stop method to eyeball where we had been and where we were headed. It is also helpful in determining the scope of work. If the project is too big, a branch of the flow diagram can end with "to be developed."

There are a couple of options. Create your straw version from scratch or find a seed guideline and modify it with your ideals including local considerations, etc. (And it should go without saying at this point that this is a **placeholder** and, that everything based on medical science for an intervention, must be critically appraised for reliability.)

We highly recommend this as a strategy and have found that this works well for other key elements, as well, such as patient hand-outs.

Go to the **Reader Resource** web page to see an example of a completed guideline algorithm (see the **Sample Projects** links).

Phase 4. Evidence Identification, Selection & Review

Again, it is not the scope of this book to teach how to evaluate the medical evidence for reliability and clinical usefulness. For those of you who *do* want to learn the basics, there is a lot of helpful information online including a lot of information freely available on our website at www.delfini.org. We also have a short book available:

> BASICS FOR EVALUATING MEDICAL RESEARCH STUDIES:
> A Simplified Approach—And Why Your Patients Need You To Know This
>
> Delfini Group Evidence-based Practice Series

Because of the vital importance of this issue, however, we will give you some important supporting advice. We will start first with an overall viewpoint.

Overall Process Highlights: The 5 "A"s—An EBM Framework

One framework for guiding evidence-based medicine work is **Ask, Acquire, Appraise, Apply and A's Again**—or the **5 "A"s of EBM** [modified from Leung]. The "Ask" is setting up your clinical question. "Acquire" is how you go about getting information. "Appraise" is evaluating that information for likely reliability and likely clinical usefulness. "Apply" is how you are going to put it all together. And "A"s again is to emphasize that information needs to be updated.

Some brief highlights with greater details coming up—

Ask

We've already addressed this, but for the sake of continuity we will repeat. Your starting point is your question. Constructing the clinical question will drive the shape of your review and the resulting information. Be clear about your focus and be clear about your scope.

Acquire

Frequently, you are threatened with being swamped with tons of information—and much of it bad. You also risk missing key puzzle pieces. How do you head for the most likely reliable and clinically useful information most efficiently? We will give you tips in the section below **Phase 4. Step 2. Identify Potentially Useful Evidence**.

Appraise: The EBM Information Quest—Is it true? Is it useful? Is it usable?™

There are three key steps to **Appraise**—and these are somewhat in order—but just as detective work is not linear, an efficient validity detective moves between the three. These are **internal validity, meaningful clinical benefit** and **external validity**.

1. Internal Validity

Critical appraisal is a core activity of evidence-based medicine (EBM) and, as we have stated, means the evaluation of medical research for its likely reliability and its clinical usefulness. In this effort, you are a validity detective, trying to establish whether associations between an intervention and an outcome are due to cause and effect (is it likely to be true?)—or whether study bias, such as lack of blinding, or chance explain or distort results. This first step is an evaluation of "internal validity," which means understanding how true the study is in its own context. (When we say "validity," we will be referring to internal validity, unless we state otherwise.)

As we have already described, training in critical appraisal is beyond the scope of this book. We will, however, include as an **Appendix** the **Delfini Short Critical Appraisal Checklist—Interventions For Prevention, Screening & Therapy** completed as a sample critical appraisal. The actual (blank) checklist itself is downloadable from the **Reader Resource** web page. This checklist should be considered to be in shorthand and so it is not explanatory. However, it will give you a one-place itemization of the essential core concepts of critical appraisal for these types of studies. (At the web page, we also provide some trainee resources.)

2. Meaningful Clinical Benefit

Another key step is assessing whether the results are likely to be useful. To be useful, you are looking for results that are likely to result in meaningful clinical benefit. Also, be aware that there is a large amount of research that does not result in meaningful clinical benefit. A reminder that clinical usefulness is a combination of a clinically meaningful outcome and the size of the study results.

A reminder that clinically meaningful outcomes are those that benefit patients the clinically meaningful outcomes are 1) morbidity; 2) mortality; 3) symptom relief; 4) mental, physical and emotional functioning; and, 5) health-related quality of life. Any other outcome is an intermediate marker and requires a causal "proof of evidence" chain that it truly provides benefit to patients in a clinically meaningful outcome.

3. External Validity

An important consideration is "external validity." External validity addresses how true the results are likely to be in medical practice— and, for this, your assessment should take into account how medicine is practiced in the context of your culture. Considerations include the study population as compared to the population of patients, as well as circumstances for care, as we have described earlier.

Again, these steps should not necessarily be thought of as linear, but as part of a package of considerations in your attempt to reach "closeness to truth"—

and some steps may get you there faster than others. For example, it is useful to do a quick assessment of both **the potential for** meaningful clinical benefit and external validity before the potentially bigger journey of taking on a validity assessment. But be careful to consider this only a peek at what may be misleading information. Do not get hoodwinked into the trap of coming to a conclusion like that of one of our student reviewers, who summarized their review of an invalid study by saying, "...despite so many threats to validity, the investigators were still able to show..." NO they were not. They "reported" benefit of an agent—and the results were highly likely to be the result of bias and not truth.

Apply

In order to apply critically appraised information, groups need to create an evidence synthesis and package the evidence and recommendations which we sometimes summarize as information aids, decision aids and action aids.

A's Again

A process should be created for periodic updating of information.

Process Steps for Phase 4. Evidence Identification, Selection & Review

There are 4 general process steps for **Phase 4. Evidence Identification, Selection & Review**. These steps are—

1. Compiling **background information**;

2. Identifying potentially useful **scientific evidence**;

3. **Critically appraising** that evidence for validity and evaluating the **usefulness of results**; and,

4. **Synthesizing and summarizing** the evidence.

The synthesized and summarized information will then be utilized for **Phase 5. Clinical Content Development**.

Phase 4. Process Step 1. Compile Background Information

a) **General background** includes, for example, current state, new evidence and future state. Some background information may be local considerations or gaps and some may be about conditions, interventions, new developments, etc.

b) **Intervention background** information. If a drug is under consideration, this includes FDA information, pharmacology, etc.

c) **Measurement instruments and interpretations**—frequently your best source for this information may be your local clinical specialist or a web search. We find it useful to identify, in advance of doing critical appraisal work, what appear to be the standard measurement instruments for any clinical question (e.g., the Beck Depression Inventory [Beck]).

   "Validated instrument" implies an instrument is valid. However, it can sometimes be a low bar for an instrument to be able to "earn" this designation.

   At a minimum, any use of a non-standard instrument should be critically appraised. Review the references in the study utilizing the instrument to identify the validation study.

d) **Representation in clinical practice guidelines**—note we said "representation" which does not mean that the clinical guideline is reliable. It must be critically appraised to discern that. A tool is available at the **Reader Resource** web page for use in critically appraising secondary sources. Whether the guideline has been effectively critically appraised using a rigorous process and its resulting grade should be made clear. Otherwise, a cautionary note should be added.

e) **Expert commentary**—generally this will be information you gather from your local clinicians, but at times this may include information that you might obtain via a web search or through some other means such as a search of another source such as the Cochrane Collaboration database.

f) **Local perspectives**—this is shorthand for whatever else it is that you need to gather (other than the evidence) that may be unique to your circumstances. This would include judgments about likely health outcomes in your population, patient and clinician perspectives and satisfaction, and other "triangulation issues" as described in **Phase 2. Clinical Improvement Project Selection > Feasibility**.

The **Reader Resource** web page contains a list of resources from our picks of "most trusted" secondary sources that can provide some of this background information—a reminder that our standard cautionary caveats about potential variability in sources applies.

Phase 4. Process Step 2. Identify Potentially Useful Evidence

Using your focused clinical question, the next step will be to attempt to identify potentially useful scientific evidence using a **systematic search** process. We will present you with some useful tips in the section, **Appendix B: Interview Questions to Help You Determine Evidence-based Know-how and Sophistication > Question: Systematic Searching**—which might be useful to look at as there are greater details and technical information there that we are not going to cover here. We also include some specific searching help at the **Reader Resource** web page. We strongly urge the review of these tools we have mentioned as we are going to keep our comments here very brief.

Before you begin, you may want to **refine your clinical question**. Crafting a clinical question requires careful consideration because, as we have pointed out, the clinical question drives the entire review. A useful framework for contemplating a clinical question is **PICOTS** which stands for patient, intervention, comparator, outcome, timing and setting [Atkins, Guyatt]. Note that we said "contemplating" because some of these elements may or may not be useful depending upon the particular question you are trying to answer.

For example, when it comes to searching, we generally don't want to limit our yield to a specific outcome. We want all outcomes. We usually want all comparators. See our **searching tool** for more detailed information about this, but we definitely want to ensure we have employed important MeSH (Medical Subject Headings) terms in our PubMed exploration to ensure our search includes related terms to the terms we have chosen. So we usually use a 2- or even a 1-part search strategy: "condition + intervention" or simply "intervention." If we are answering an efficacy question (and initially for safety too), we limit our review to clinical trials.

We use the **titles and abstracts** to weed out studies that are not relevant, that fit our exclusion criteria or which we can determine on the spot are obviously lethally threatened (meaning are not likely to be reliable due to an important bias or chance problem).

Keeping immediate **documentation of each search** is *vital* and—while one of those less "appreciated" tasks, such as filing—not doing so can lead one to being embroiled in a disastrous mess if not attended to just-in-time which may be impossible to untangle or replicate later on if need be. We will provide you with documentation advice at the **Reader Resource** web page.

As described in **Interview Questions**, an efficient way to find high-quality information may be to start with the most potentially reliable systematic reviews.

Another important tip is to **review the references** in the articles you retrieve. Sometimes important articles are found this way. Be sure to create documentation of any references you obtain through these "hand-searches" so that you can include them in your search documentation.

Phase 4. Process Step 3. Critically Appraise Studies for Validity and Usefulness of Results

Important reminder: *All* primary and secondary study information **must be critically appraised**. At our **Reader Resource** web page, we include links to critical appraisal tools for primary and secondary studies and for secondary sources.

Studies and other sources must be assessed for relevance to the clinical question; for uncertainty of, or threats to, validity; and, for clinical usability to determine which studies should be excluded from further consideration.

As stated before, it is beyond the scope of this book to teach critical appraisal concepts. There are many resources available to help you including those found at our website at http://www.delfini.org. The **Reader Resource** web page includes both selections from our web site as well as tools, but there is much more information freely available to you directly on our main website.

A Reminder of What Critical Appraisal is About

A reminder that the goal of critical appraisal is to help assess whether a study is likely to be—

- **True**.

- If likely to be true, is it **clinically useful**?

Importantly, we stress again that critical appraisal is much less about evaluating statistics than it is about **identifying threats to validity** ("closeness" to truth) by identifying the potential for **bias** (something systematically leading away from truth) or **chance** (a random occurrence). It is only with knowledge about the validity of the study that we can appropriately assess whether the reported results are likely to be reasonable estimates of effect or are likely to be distorted by study flaws.

Performing critical appraisal combines three attributes to try and answer, "What explains the results: bias, chance or truth?"—in this case of interventions, truth = cause & effect:

- **Critical thinking**;

- Understanding essential **critical appraisal concepts** (which are often critical thinking shortcuts that someone else has already thought through); and,

- **Clinical knowledge**.

Authors' Conclusions Are Opinions

One more caution we will add is that authors' conclusions are not evidence; authors' conclusions are opinions. And as we have stated before, everyone involved in research should be assumed to have a bias.

There are two main ways evidence reviews can be conducted. You do it or someone else does it. If the latter, you need ways to assess their reliability. For many reasons, including the likelihood that it will be challenging to find reliable outside information, it is possible that you will want to take this task on directly. Again, it is not the scope of this book to teach you critical appraisal—there are other resources for that—but we will provide you with some methodological information if you are going to take this route—which frequently we would recommend.

If Your Own Team Will Review the Evidence...

As we have stated, we will provide you with some resources at the **Reader Resource** web page that are more likely to be reliable, to our knowledge, than other sources. But you may wish to review the evidence yourself—which is a very reasonable choice given the state of health care information.

If you are going to do this, it is recommended that you provide training to your team or supporting staff. Usually, team members will need highly skilled individuals, frequently evidence-based subject matter experts or librarians, to do the searching. However, most librarians need training in evidence-based approaches—otherwise, you may be swamped with information unlikely to be reliable, such as case series. In some cases, pharmacists, nurses, physicians and others who are skilled in evidence-based principles can perform the searches if librarians are not available.

We will share with you some of our approaches.

Before We Begin Our Reviews: Mapping the "Ideal" Study

One strategy that we have sometimes found useful before starting our critical appraisal work on a project is to outline selected key components of an ideal study to guide us as a benchmark when reviewing the individual selected studies. The operative word here is "guide." Generally, we do not use this information to create hard and fast rules for accepting studies, but it gives us some useful comparative information as we start out and also as we make discoveries along the way. This can also be a helpful strategy when multiple people are engaged in a single review or when training new staff and may be useful to share with the project team during the meeting for that review.

Again, we do not always do this step, and when we do, we do not necessarily research all of this information—but a selection of some parameters that we have found helpful is available at the **Reader Resource** web page: see the downloadable **Delfini Ideal Study Parameters Tool.** Considerations include items such as ideals for the clinical question to be considered, comparator, population for study, dosing, pharmacology information, ideal treatment and follow-up length, ideal diagnosis methods and measurement methods and tools, etc.

When using this approach, the ideals may become modified along the way as new learnings occur. For example, in the middle of a review of triptans, we discovered a unique challenge in making a placebo that tasted as foul as the study triptan which was a nasal preparation. Upon this discovery and the potential for risk of unblinding subjects and their physicians, we updated our ideals sheet and checked back to see what other reviews we had done using this agent to update potential threats to validity.

How We Conduct Our Critical Appraisal Reviews

Some Critical Appraisal Tips

Transparency is an important hallmark of evidence-based clinical decision-making. Therefore, you need a process for **documenting** critical appraisal findings, which should be supplied to team members and kept for records. There are a number of choices for appraisal process and documentation activities. Having performed thousands (and possibly tens-of-thousands) of critical appraisals and trying out different methods, we will share with you our favorites, and then give you some varying methods that we frequently recommend to groups. You will want to find methods that work best for you and your particular needs and circumstances. A reminder again that there are exceptions to everything we say.

It's Not About Being Fair to the Authors or Accommodating Reality Challenges; It's About Being Fair About Truth: Strengths versus Weaknesses

Before we talk about our methods, however, we need to make a key point about critical appraisal. To determine the likely reliability of the study, you need to **rule out bias and chance as possible explanations for reported study results**. This means that critical appraisal necessarily **focuses on the negative**.

Positive aspects about a study do not "balance" out negatives—they can only mitigate them. Doing a critical appraisal is not akin to doing an employee evaluation in which you identify positive aspects and areas needing work to create a balanced look at an employee's performance. Critical appraisal is more akin to building a house where a beautiful viewpoint cannot make up for the problems of building on quicksand.

One study problem alone may be significant enough to create doubts about reported study results. Or it may be that a series of problems or uncertainties result in sufficient concern that a study should be rejected as being at **high or uncertain risk of bias**. Explicit details must be provided by the author. It is insufficient for an author to use the term "double-blind" in the title of a study and not provide details of how blinding was performed. When details are not provided, the critical appraisal findings should be "**uncertain risk of bias**."

Also, keep ever focused on the goal of critical appraisal which is to discern **whether reported study results are likely to be true or not**. The bar for validity does not get lowered because of realistic challenges such as in our earlier example of the difficulty of masking the taste of a nasal triptan. Authors are not being graded for their good intentions; molecules should not be blessed with a good grade because they are "beautiful;" problems such as "it was not possible to blind" are not to be "forgiven." Evidence grading is not about authors' efforts and challenges: reliability of information is.

Because we are trying to answer the question, "**Are the reported results likely to be true?**," many times we can reach a conclusion that a study is of sufficiently high risk of bias or uncertain risk of bias that we can terminate our review without assessing many of the study elements. Again, sometimes a study is lethally threatened by only one threat. Therefore, an efficiency is to only **critically appraise a study as far as you need to**. Meaning, if a study is going to end up being rejected, you want to discern that as quickly as possible. This is not to imply that you should be too hasty in your judgment. This is to say that you **may choose to document threats to validity only so far as you need** to in order to determine whether the study is usable or not.

The **Delfini Short Critical Appraisal Checklist: Interventions for Prevention, Screening & Therapy,** downloadable at both our website and the **Reader Resource** web page, provides a comprehensive list of critical appraisal items to review. We will hereinafter refer to this as the "**short critical appraisal checklist**."

Our Favored Processes: How We Read a Study

A joke that we frequently tell our workshop participants is that when we "read a study," we don't really read the study! (Actually, the true answer is "it depends"—but, in any event, our approach is very different than sitting down and reading an article from start to finish.) We each have a slightly different way that works most happily for us individually. Mike likes to review a study online. Sheri likes to print out a copy of the article for review. In both instances, we make notations right on the document. Doing so results in instant documentation, plus it makes it very easy to engage in study discussions because it is very easy to find key study information. Mike likes to use a structured approach; Sheri prefers efficiency. Different reviewers may prefer one method over another or take a different approach.

Mike & The "Name That Bias" Approach

Mike likes using a framework. He likes to organize his findings, at a minimum, in the categories of selection, performance, data/attrition and assessment biases; chance; and, results (both efficacy and safety). In addition, he likes to make a summary statement regarding the risk of bias and a grade for both efficacy and safety. In reviewing the study, he is looking for specific critical appraisal items such as prespecified outcomes, treatment duration, population for study, methods to allocate patients to their study groups, blinding, performance differences, safety population, etc. In short, the items from our short checklist.

When Mike starts his review, he attaches a note or a comment at the start of the electronic copy of the article, listing the categories mentioned above as headers within the note. When he finds a critical appraisal item, he attaches a new note or comment to tag that item (e.g., "duration"), linking that note to the location of the information about that item in the document. This way, he has created a map of sorts of the various critical appraisal items of interest. As he finds threats to validity, he goes to his first note and enters the threat under the appropriate category. For example, if he identifies a problem about the study population, he enters that information very briefly in his first note under the category, **Selection Bias**. This way he has a very organized and uniform approach.

He *always* checks his work by a quick run through of our **short critical appraisal checklist** to ensure he has not missed anything—especially anything not otherwise mentioned in the article.

Sheri & "A Bias by Any Other Name Is Still a Bias"

Sheri approaches a project differently. Sheri takes a printed copy of the article and, pen in hand, makes abbreviated notes in the extreme margins of her hard copy. When she notices information about randomization, she writes RAND. When she notices information about blinding, she writes BLND. The point is that she moves very quickly to simply map locations for key items to be critically appraised in the margins. When it comes time to make an assessment about blinding, for example, she can quickly spot all instances of blinding information reported in the study to evaluate them collectively.

If she notices any problem during this quick fast pass, she will add a minus sign (and sometimes a plus sign if a potential strength may mitigate a bias). Depending on the specific issues with study quality, sometimes she is done with the article at this point. If she needs to go back to re-review any items, it is easy to do a quick scan down her margins. This method is certainly not as formal as Mike's, but comparatively it is very fast.

She *always* checks her work by a quick run through of our **short critical appraisal checklist**. You'll notice a theme here. Even though we are very experienced reviewers, you risk missing something not even mentioned in a study without a validity checklist. *We, too, are likely to miss what is not there.* **Always, use a validity checklist.**

How We Document Our Critical Appraisal Findings

We have found it very efficient to copy the study abstract from PubMed into a word processing document, add anything that we feel should have been included in the abstract or anything of note (FYI, it is rare that we add anything—and when we do we make sure to tag it as being added by us), and then we list our threats to validity and our assigned grade or evidence conclusion.

If we determine that the study is valid, we then add key efficacy and safety results if information is needed in addition to the abstract.

For studies that are not valid or are of uncertain validity, if we have found useful safety information, we include that along with standard safety cautions, which we will describe. To describe the context of the study and key study elements (useful for external validity considerations and also for determining what studies might be reasonable to consider in aggregate when summarizing findings about an intervention), we also might make additional study notes using **PICOTS** (again, patient, intervention, comparator, outcome, timing and setting), adding an additional "P" to the mix (**PICPOTS**), standing for "performance outcomes" such as adherence outcomes or special contextual elements of the care experienced by study subjects.

Typical Delfini Critical Appraisal Documentation

1. Citation including PubMed PMID number

2. Date of review and reviewer

3. Abstract from PubMed

4. Reviewer additions (meaning any additions we think are important in addition to the abstract—again, we rarely add anything)

5. Threats to validity

6. Other comments

7. Evidence grade or tag and conclusion

8. Valid efficacy results

9. Key safety results and safety grade with cautionary notes (we will give you an example, and we will give you more information on assessing safety in the section, **Phase 4. Process Step 4. Synthesize and Summarize the Evidence**)

10. Potentially **PICPOTS** elements (population, intervention, comparator, performance outcomes, study outcomes, timing and setting)

11. Any other key comments

Again, in the **Appendix**, we will provide you a hypothetical example of what a critical appraisal might look like.

Our Favored Processes: Evidence Grading

Evidence grading is simply a tag of a **summary conclusion** about the quality of a study or other item or element such as a body of evidence, a clinical guideline or a clinical recommendation, for example. At times, we rate the "body of evidence" and refer to it as the overall "strength of evidence" (SOE), a concept that we will discuss again in the section, **Phase 4. Process Step 4. Synthesize and Summarize the Evidence**.

Whenever you see an evidence grade, it is vitally important that you make sure you **understand the criteria** for achieving a specific grade. Many grading systems may use similar words, but have very different criteria. And unfortunately, many criteria upgrade trials so that trials may be given a high grade when in fact they are not valid.

We have a very simple system, the criteria for which essentially are your judgment about the distorting effects of bias and chance and your assessment of clinical significance. The Delfini grading system is designed to be easy to understand, easy to remember and flexible to apply. The concepts behind our grading system can be applied to individual studies, outcomes or conclusions from studies, systematic reviews, clinical recommendations, guidelines, etc. Most frequently, we grade studies, outcomes and SOE using a system of A, B, B-U or U. We use A, B and B-U to inform efficacy decisions. Grade U evidence is rarely used by us to inform efficacy decisions, but may be used for safety, but with cautionary statements that the evidence is of uncertain reliability. Our grading tool is available at our website and also at the **Reader Resource** web page. To summarize—

Grade A: Useful

The evidence is strong and appears sufficient to use in making health care decisions—it is both valid and useful (e.g., meets standards for clinical significance, sufficient magnitude of effect size, physician and patient acceptability, etc.). Studies achieving this grade should be outstanding in design, methodology, execution and reporting and have successful study performance outcomes, providing useful information to aid clinical decision-making, enabling reasonable certitude in drawing conclusions.

For a body of evidence: Several well-designed and conducted studies that consistently show similar results.

For therapy, screening and prevention: RCTs. In some cases a single, large Grade A RCT may be sufficient; however, without confirmation from other studies, results could be due to chance, undetected significant biases, fraud, etc. In such instance, the SOE should include a cautionary note.

Grade A should be rarely assigned to any study. ("Extra points" are not given for challenge or difficulty in answering the research question. Authors should not be given extra points by second-guessing them. Transparency is required.)

Grade B: Possibly Useful

Grade B studies should be very well designed and executed and meet most of the requirements that it takes to achieve a Grade A. Grade B evidence appears potentially strong and is probably sufficient to use in making health care decisions—some threats to validity have been identified. Studies achieving this grade should be of high quality and contain only non-lethal threats to validity and with sufficiently useful information to aid clinical decision-making, enabling reasonable certitude in drawing conclusions.

For a body of evidence: The evidence is strong enough to conclude that the results are probably valid and useful (see above); however, study results from multiple studies are inconsistent or the studies may have some (but not lethal) threats to validity.

For therapy, screening and prevention: RCTs. In some cases a single, large Grade B RCT may be sufficient; however, without confirmation from other studies results could be due to chance, undetected significant biases, fraud, etc. In such instance, the SOE should include a cautionary note.

Grade B is more frequent than Grade A, but is still a difficult grade to achieve.

Grade B-U: Possible to Uncertain Usefulness

The evidence might be sufficient to use in making health care decisions; however, there remains sufficient uncertainty that the evidence cannot fully reach a Grade B, and the uncertainty is not great enough to fully warrant a Grade U.

Grade U: Uncertain Validity and/or Usefulness

There is sufficient uncertainty that caution is urged regarding its use in making health care decisions. Grade U should be assigned when there is sufficient uncertainty about the accuracy of the estimates of effect resulting in an inability to comfortably draw conclusions from the research and in comfortably applying results.

We end up assigning most studies a Grade U. As stated, we generally never use Grade U studies to inform efficacy decisions, but we will use Grade U evidence for safety, being very careful to describe that the evidence is of low quality.

For readers who would like more detailed information about other systems, a good place to start is a publication from the Agency for Healthcare and Research and Quality (AHRQ) and the online Cochrane Handbook [Owens, Higgins]. We also have additional information available at our website.

Documenting an Appraisal Your Way

You might wish to adopt a fairly spare approach such as ours—but frequently we recommend that groups consider creating a **critical appraisal template** that is complete and instructive. The advantages of our short approach that we have just described are that it is quick to complete, and it is fairly easy to review the threats to validity. Conversely, the advantage of a more detailed templatized approach is that it can be constructed in such a way as to remind members of key appraisal considerations which otherwise might be forgotten or misunderstood, can be used for training and standardization, and it is easy for someone auditing the appraisal to ensure all key critical appraisal elements have been considered, as well as for members to know where to go for key appraisal information.

Using **Selection Bias** as an example, the template questions might go something like this:

1. Potential biases that might result from the population studied (review inclusions, exclusions and baseline characteristics)

2. Potential biases that might result from how subjects were selected for study

3. Concerns with sample size

4. Concerns with group assignment (review assignment method such as details of randomization and concealment of allocation of subjects to their study group—address each issue)

5. Any noted imbalance between groups

Be sure to **document your methods used to determine validity and usability**—this should be part of the supporting information in your monograph/review.

At the **Reader Resource** web page, we have included links for several downloadable Delfini critical appraisal tools including a 1-pager to help learners with essential critical appraisal concepts, plus the 1-page short critical appraisal checklist. We have also included a longer guide. There is also a link to our book there which both new learners and those who are experienced with critical appraisal will find to be of help.

Critical Appraisal of Secondary Studies and Secondary Sources

EBCQI teams often seek out secondary sources such as guidelines—but all secondary studies and sources must be evaluated carefully in the same way RCTs are evaluated. Separate templates should be used to document assessments for validity.

Many systematic reviews and meta-analyses are of low quality and, unless the authors have carefully evaluated the included studies for validity, staffers will have to assess each included study.

As we have pointed out, clinical guidelines present even greater difficulty in terms of validity assessment than do systematic reviews. Many guidelines are not fully transparent, do not do a good job of evaluating the quality of the evidence and do not do a good job of linking the quality of the evidence to the strength of the recommendation [Grilli, Kuehn, Laine, Shaneyfeldt]. The same cautions hold for compendia and other secondary sources [Abernethy].

Cost-effectiveness studies are another area where secondary sources often fail to ensure that efficacy has been proved. We will provide you with more information on what you can do to accomplish cost analysis in **Phase 6. Assess Impacts of Practice Change > Critical Appraisal of Economic Cost Analysis**.

For Secondary Studies and Secondary Sources We Recommend That You Conduct a Bi-Level Review and Update: Appraise Included Research Studies + Appraise the Quality of the Methods for Creating the Secondary Study or the Secondary Source + Update With New Studies

In addition to being concerned about the validity of research studies included in a systematic review, the systematic review itself has its own specific requirements that must be critically appraised.

If any secondary source does not pass a critical appraisal audit, a source might still be usable as a basis for project if it is agreed that the **search and exclusions** have been performed rigorously. In this instance, the conclusions of the review would not be used, but rather all studies selected for inclusion in the review should be critically appraised. Any that are deemed to not be both valid and clinically useful should be discarded, and a new synthesis and summary should be developed after an update is performed.

Information from any secondary studies and sources almost always requires **updating**, which entails a search for any studies **published after the search date** (not publication date) of the systematic review and critical appraisal of those studies determined to be potentially valid and relevant.

Phase 4. Process Step 4. Synthesize and Summarize the Evidence

When the evidence has been graded for validity and clinical usefulness, the studies chosen for inclusion are tagged with evidence grades and used to create the evidence summary, also known as the "evidence synthesis." The goal of evidence synthesis is to summarize the best available valid and useful evidence into a conclusion.

SOE or Strength of the Evidence

A typical feature of evidence synthesis is to **grade the overall strength of the evidence or the SOE**. We first grade each included study for validity and clinical usefulness. We then assign an overall rating for the strength of evidence, based on our ratings of the included studies considering overall risk of bias, consistency of findings and effect size. When not grading the SOE with our A, B, B-U or U system, we use a modified version of the Agency for Healthcare Research and Quality and the Effective Health Care Program (AHRQ-EHCP) system [Owens], rating the SOE as high, moderate, borderline or inconclusive.

We rate the **SOE as high** when we have high confidence that the evidence reflects the true effect. Further research is very unlikely to change our confidence in the estimate of effect. This usually requires several well-designed and conducted studies at low risk of bias reporting similar results, although at times a single, large, well-designed and conducted study may suffice.

We rate the **SOE as moderate** when we have moderate confidence that the evidence reflects the true effect. Further research may change our confidence in the estimate of effect and may change the estimate. This usually requires several studies not at high risk of bias, but results may be inconsistent or the studies may have some (but not lethal) threats to validity. Again, at times a single, large, well-designed and conducted study may suffice.

We use the **borderline** category when the SOE falls between moderate and inconclusive. The evidence may be reliable enough to be useful in informing decisions, but caution is urged and further evidence is needed. There be may higher risk of bias or a wider range of reported effect size in the included studies.

We rate the **SOE as inconclusive** when the evidence is absent, conflicting, sparse, or weak and conclusions based on evidence cannot be drawn.

Evidence Synthesis

The evidence summary, or synthesis, is usually a text statement that includes both the **quality of the evidence** and the **strength of the conclusion or recommendation**. Language that is inaccurate, misleading or vague, such as "Recent evidence suggests..." or "There is evidence that..." should be avoided. It is recommended that the statement include any limitations of the drug review and subsequent synthesis.

There is no one correct way to synthesize the evidence—you'll have to apply judgment. Quantitative information should be included. Here's an example of an evidence synthesis statement:

Fictional Example of Evidence Synthesis: Myoceptimab for Angina Pectoris

The strength of the evidence (SOE), based on two large, valid RCTs, is sufficient to conclude that, in patients with multivessel coronary artery disease untreatable by percutaneous coronary intervention (PCI), myoceptimab reduces a combination of cardiovascular disease outcomes (overall mortality, cardiovascular death, non-fatal myocardial infarction and refractory angina risk) when compared to placebo over a three year period. The relative risk (RR) for the combined endpoint is 0.58, 95% confidence interval 0.51 to 0.73, $p<0.001$. Absolute risk reduction (ARR) is 4%, 95% CI 2.53% to 5.36%. The NNT is 25, 95% CI 19 to 40 (SOE: High)

You will notice that the evidence synthesis statement is very **evidence-focused**. Keep this summary very scientific. In **Phase 5. Clinical Content Development**, you will adapt the evidence synthesis statement for project application. At this stage, however, you want it to remain pure to your evidence findings. Doing so enables this to be reference material as you might want to make application changes later on, need this for documentation purposes, may need it for justification, etc.

It is also useful to include in the evidence synthesis some aggregated information obtained from your **search documentation** about the studies used to create the monograph or class review, such as the number of included studies, number of patients, population characteristics, homogeneity/ heterogeneity of studies included, etc. **PICPOTS** can be useful to you here.

Safety Data

Evaluating **safety** data is a complex process. Adverse events often occur infrequently and are usually not prespecified as outcome measures in RCTs— which means they may be at high risk of being chance effects. Also, they may be detected long after completion of RCTs through observational reports. It may be reasonable at times to use safety data from lower-quality RCTs, because safety information from selected lower-grade RCTs may have greater validity and usefulness than observational studies or case reports generated after RCTs are completed. However, it may be necessary to incorporate observational information into safety information if potentially significant risks are detected following the publication of an RCT. FDA post-marketing safety data may also be useful. As with efficacy data, safety data should be appraised for quality and assigned an evidence grade. When safety outcomes are not prespecified, it can be useful to look for patterns across multiple studies to decrease the likelihood of drawing conclusions based on chance effects.

Conclusions about risks should be worded carefully so that information drawn from potentially flawed data regarding risks is not presented as if it is based on stronger research than actually exists. Although a study may be rated low quality overall, it may be sufficiently valid in one area, such as safety. Therefore, at times, it may be worthwhile to grade individual study conclusions rather than to assign a grade to the overall study.

More Help For Evidence Synthesis

See the 1-pager + the long tool on evidence synthesis at the **Reader Resource** web page for more information, along with the evidence grading tool (long version) which includes suggested language for **wording conclusions**, including some wording that we use for standard safety precautions.

Documentation

It is important to document the search sources, search terms, inclusion and exclusion criteria for studies. A flowchart for summarizing the search results and application of inclusion criteria is also recommended. The methods for initially assessing the studies and the subsequent assessment of relevant studies should be documented. Details of evidence grading should be included.

Phase 5. Clinical Content Development

In Phase 5, your team will **draft** the **basis** for the **project's ideal clinical content**. The evidence synthesis is a key component of this work. However, whereas the evidence synthesis statement is a scientific summary, what you use for clinical content may be somewhat different. This is a "knowledge transfer" phase where you take the scientific assessment and consider how you wish to apply it to your project.

We emphasize "**draft**" as you may make significant changes after **Phase 6. Assess Impacts of Practice Change**. We emphasize "**basis**" as many outputs may be issued from your clinical content statements to serve many target audiences and many needs. We emphasize "**context**" as there may be some differences which may occur due to population differences, limited availability of resources, weakness of evidence in which case you may need to supplement content with local expert opinion from your team, etc. And so a key activity in this phase will be to contemplate your evidence synthesis and move it from a more purely scientific form to how you are going to apply the information. And when we say move it from a more "purely scientific form," this may simply mean that you restate the science in a more accessible way.

Thus, this is an "interpretive," "translational," "adaptive," and "applied" activity **based on the specifics of your project** which includes its **context within your organization**. In thinking through your approach, you will want to consider your organization's own requirements, both generally and specific to this project. These include your organization's needs and problems, special circumstances, values and preferences, etc., all of which go into informing its **goals** and **realities**. We will refer to this as your **organizational priorities**.

In an ideal world, organization priorities *are* **priorities for patient-centered care**. A reminder, patient-centered care means attention to accommodating the **personal health care requirements of individual patients**. This includes (and you will note the parallels to the organization's considerations above) a patient's own personal health care problems, special circumstances, values and preferences, all of which go into informing his or her **health care needs** and **wants**.

The clinical content will ultimately be finalized in **Phase 7. Communication Tools Development** and can be used to create a variety of helpful clinical improvement products such as those listed in that section at **Examples of Clinical Communication Tools**. You may wish to skip ahead to peruse that list **at some point during this stage** as you plan your next steps.

You created clinical questions; now you want to supply some answers. Therefore, in planning your clinical content, a first step is typically to move your evidence into a set of **clinical recommendations**.

Clinical Recommendations

Your starting point for your potential array of communications is likely to be a clinical recommendation or a set of recommendations, and ideally, you have reliable and clinically useful evidence to inform and construct them.

Ideally, clinical recommendations are statements designed to optimize patient care. Your **evidence synthesis** + **patient health care requirements** + **organizational priorities** are all part of your work creating clinical recommendations. In Delfini's idealized world, evidence trumps organizational priorities and patient requirements trump organizational priorities—yet we all have to live in the real world, and so we advise you to do the best that you can, always keeping the patient in mind.

In most instances, clinical recommendations will include the evidence synthesis and team recommendations—both tagged with ratings. The same concepts behind our grading system can be applied to rating of recommendations.

Recommendations should be crisp with clarity about the population, the SOE and the action to be taken. Example—

RECOMMENDED ACTION: Add Myoceptimab for treatment of angina in patients aged 55 and older with a history of coronary heart disease or exercise-related angina and who do not have a diagnosis of heart failure.
• Strength of evidence: High with NNT 5 (3 yrs), 95% CI (3 to 7) synthesized in studied populations • Safety: no known issues, but standard safety cautions apply especially with new agents • Strength of recommendation: Strong

Phase 6. Assess Impacts of Practice Change

In this phase, you will—

1. Anticipate the impacts of change for the organization including impacts on health, cost and satisfaction;

2. Re-consider feasibility issues;

3. Decide if the quality improvement project will be implemented;

4. If yes, decide upon the plan of action including managing the impacts of change;

5. Explore what may be needed for sustainability; and,

6. Make content changes as needed. Rinse and repeat, as they say...

Largely, these steps speak for themselves, but here are a few details on **Step 1. Anticipate the Impacts of Change**...

Assessing Impacts of Practice Change: Simple Description

Simply put, assessing impacts of practice change involves comparing current practices to what you propose to change with the goal of predicting any possible future outcomes. The goal here is to think very broadly about anything that might be a result of change, i.e., both positive and negative outcomes. We will break this down in greater detail in **But It Is Not Just About Cost.**

Let us give you a simple example. At Group Health Cooperative, where we worked, our organization was primarily a provider of care and secondarily an insurer for our own provision of care. For companies that are not actually providing care, a frequent concern of practice change resulting from EBCQI team decisions involves how policy changes may be negatively perceived by patients and their care providers. Therefore, this often is—and should be—a focal point for attention. So part of the change assessment impact could be to—

1. Acknowledge the potential for negative perception;

2. Reconsider feasibility; and,

3. If still deciding to implement the change—

4. Develop communication strategies about changes to patients and their clinicians as part of the implementation action plan.

Tip: If the change is due to the evidence, helping to educate about that, including quantitative information, can be useful. Keep in mind that, with many providers and patients, you will be breaking new ground—so focus your messaging on both the evidence for your recommended clinical change as well as general information about the importance of an evidence-based approach.

It's not all about cost, but let's start with cost as that is often a chief consideration in assessing impacts of practice change.

Economic Analysis Methods: Basics

There are many useful economic analysis tools, and selecting the most useful tool or tools will vary, depending upon the published evidence, the knowledge and skills of those responsible for evaluating the economic analysis and the needs of the organization. Below we have summarized the most-frequently used economic analysis methods. Another helpful tool is the "balance sheet" approach, which we describe after we address considerations other than cost.

1. Cost-Analysis

This is the simplest analysis and considers the cost of interventions, e.g., drugs, but may include the costs of a treatment or drug program (see

Balance Sheet discussion below). The analysis usually includes a comparison to alternatives. This may be the limit of what some groups can or will choose to do. In this case, the other triangulation variables such as amount of benefit, etc., can be discussed at the meeting.

2. Cost-Benefit Analysis

Cost-benefit analysis gives consideration to the cost/outcomes of an intervention alone or compared to alternatives. The numbers-needed-to-treat (NNT) for various options can be compared, but care must be taken to consider differences in the evidence available for the various options. For example, various **PICPOTS** elements and more (study populations, treatment durations, dosages, co-interventions and other contextual issues, study endpoints, biases, study performance outcomes, etc.) must be considered before comparing NNTs.

3. Cost-Effectiveness Analysis (CEA)

The ratio of net cost/health outcome for the agents of interest—also known as the cost effectiveness ratio (CER)—can be calculated and compared, but this method requires that the same effectiveness measures are used with the various interventions.

4. Cost-Utility Analysis

The goal of cost-utility analysis is to determine the cost per quality adjusted life year (QALY) saved. QALYs include both the quantity (e.g., survival time differences) and the quality (utilities) of the outcomes.

Published cost-utility analyses are frequently flawed because authors frequently fail to critically appraise the studies upon which variables such as the time in various health states and other outcomes are based. Instead, they frequently simply accept the reported study outcomes. They then create models using acquisition cost data, utility data and assumptions about various processes of care which are built into the model.

An important problem with this method is the determination of the utilities. To create the numerical values for utilities, the investigators must first define the health states of interest (e.g., metastatic disease without progression, progression, terminal state). Then they must assign values between 0 (death) and 1 (full health) to the disease states in order to establish the utilities. This is frequently done through use of time trade-offs, standard gambles and visual analogue scales. In many cases, surrogate raters (i.e., the general population, specialists) assign the numerical values because it is difficult to obtain ratings from patients who may be in very poor health. Furthermore, utilities may vary greatly between individuals.

To derive quality-adjusted life-years (QALYs) saved —and the incremental cost-effectiveness ratio (ICER)—models are used. ICER is an equation which creates a ratio of the change in costs to incremental benefits of a therapeutic intervention or treatment. The equation for ICER is—

$$\text{ICER} = (C1 - C2) / (E1 - E2)$$

C1 and E1 are the cost and effect in the intervention or treatment group. C2 and E2 are the cost and effect in the control group. Costs are usually described in monetary units while benefits/effect in health status is measured in terms of QALYs gained or lost.

Participants who evaluate and summarize cost-utility studies will need to determine if their organization's cost numbers are similar to those included in the model and whether the studies used for outcomes are valid. They will need to assess the assumptions used in the model, whether the model included the relevant outcomes such as adverse events, whether real-world outcomes are likely to be similar to the outcomes in the RCTs included in the model and whether they agree with the methods utilized and the results reported for the utilities before accepting the reported QALY data.

And none of this should be done until studies used for the analyses have been critically appraised and determined to be valid. We make our health care analysis study critical appraisal tool available via a link at the **Reader Resource** web page.

But It Is Not Just About Cost

We gave you a fairly simple description of assessing impacts of practice change at the beginning of our discussion about this phase. At its most basic level, cost is easy to think about: what is it costing us now and what will it cost to change and sustain the change? Ideally, however, you look at impacts of change beyond cost and for that, a deeper description of what this phase is about, may be helpful.

Assessing Impacts of Practice Change: Details

The goal of this phase is to identify what is going on currently (current state), attempt to project what is likely to change with close attention to the positive and the negative (changed state), what is likely to be needed to cause desired change to happen (implementation), what is likely to be needed to maintain change (change maintenance), and what is needed for measurement and reporting.

In list form, these are—

1. Assessment of the **current state** in various categorical areas;

2. Projection of potential changes (positive, neutral and negative) for the **changed state**;

3. Plan for what you can do to achieve the desired changed state by way of **implementation**;

4. What are you likely to need to do to **maintain** the change?; and,

5. How will you **measure** and **report** outcomes?

When assessing impacts of practice change, **pay attention** to the items listed in **Phase 2. Clinical Improvement Project Selection > Feasibility**, such as various considerations about what may change (such as health care outcomes, satisfaction, resources, capacity, etc., and including triangulation issues); whether you have structures, systems and processes in place; work culture issues, etc.

To provide you with a simple example, at Group Health, Mike's team facilitated the development of a dysuria clinical guideline targeting healthy women without risk factors, eliminating the pre-treatment urinalysis, culture and visit. Women who met the criteria for being at low risk of an ascending urinary tract infection could pick up their prescriptions and treat the episode of dysuria without a clinic visit. A system/role/skill change included triaging calls, as appropriate, to our Consulting Nurse Service and providing training and a protocol for the staff nurses. Another change was creating an order set for the new prescription standard.

Looking strictly at satisfaction, we predicted that patients would be very satisfied. However, we anticipated that clinicians would probably experience some dissatisfaction because the visits for low risk acute dysuria are usually short, giving them some catch-up time in their schedules. In considering implementation activities, this project might invite something like a special communication to affected providers helping them appreciate the value of this change to patients along with a succinct review of the evidence.

You may not be performing a deep analysis of potential impacts of practice change; however, frequently there are unintended consequences of change — and you should be aware of this. The various considerations we have provided to you should give you some guidance about things to think about and discuss with others.

Balance Sheets

The **balance sheet** serves as a reminder to consider all important clinical practice changes when doing EBCQI projects. David Eddy developed this model to assist groups estimate health and economic outcomes and consequences of adopting new interventions [Eddy]. We used this model extensively at Group Health in Seattle and have described our modifications [Braddick].

A balance sheet is a simple method for **comparing** current cost and outcomes in an organization to cost and outcomes associated with a clinical practice change.

Balance sheets incorporate both local cost and process data along with evidence from the medical literature to assist in projecting impacts. They condense important information into a space that can be grasped visually and mentally at one time. Balance sheets are useful when practice changes are more complex than just adding a drug which is similar to existing alternatives.

The balance sheet serves as a reminder to consider all important clinical practice changes. Looking back at our dysuria guideline example, in order to estimate impacts of change, we created a balance sheet which included the number of women ages 18-70 years with dysuria and urgency; number of urinalyses; number of urine cultures; number of prescriptions for trimethoprim/ sulfamethoxazole, amoxicillin, cephalexin, nitrofurantoin and trimethoprim; and, adverse events (rash, vaginitis). We then obtained costs and calculated total costs. The final step was to estimate outcomes and total costs after implementing the dysuria guideline.

For interested readers, a link to more balance sheet information is available at the **Reader Resource** web page.

Phase 7. Communication Tools Development

Optimal decisions depend upon **reliable and useful information** which is a key output of *evidence-based* CQI processes. A final step before implementation is the creation of materials that will assist end-users **understand information, make decisions and take appropriate actions**. The work for this effort started in **Phase 5. Clinical Content Development**. At this stage, you move forward to create final products.

Important **target groups** should be identified and communication tools should be tailored for each group. Tools to assist users should be developed for leaders, clinicians, patients and others as appropriate and made available through **various media**, such as electronic medical records and hard copy.

Examples of Clinical Communication Tools

Example of communications tools include—

1. Algorithms or protocols;

2. Evidence syntheses and evidence statements;

3. Clinical recommendations;

4. 1-pagers and messages for clinicians;

5. Patient information;

6. Special tools for clinicians (e.g., e-messaging, decision support, formulary information, risk stratification tools, diagnostic tools); and,

7. Patient communications (information, decision and action aids).

When making decisions about your content, it is important to consider various elements. At the **Reader Resource** web page, we provide you with a tool for helping create **patient communication aids** that **can be generalized for other purposes**.

Key questions which will affect the form of the content include—

1. What do you want to **communicate** and what is the **purpose**?

2. Who is the intended **audience**?

3. How will the content be **delivered** (e.g., interpersonal, publication, internet, electronic health record, telephonic, video, etc.)?

4. How will the content **reach** and catch the **attention** of the recipient?

5. What will be the best **timing**?

An efficient method of preparing for content development is to have the evidence synthesis and the clinical recommendations in front of the team, formatted as key clinical questions with the answers. The team can then consider the needs of each target group and develop various communication aids, 1-page advisements, messaging scripts, etc.

Many examples of clinical content are available on our website at www.delfini.org.

Examples of Patient Communication Aids

More information on communication tools development and examples are available at the **Reader Resource** web page. These tools include several patient communication resources including a tool to provide you with ideas for creating patient communication aids (again, **which can be generalized for other audiences**). These include the following—

1. **Information aids**: Strictly informational pieces to help patients understand various issues, e.g., background information, diagnostic, prognostic or therapeutic information. The important point is that

the contained information should be reliable. Example, a backgrounder on osteoporosis or facts about bone density testing.

2. **Decision aids**: Informational, yet with the goal of helping a patient (and, ideally, providers too) come to a decision about choosing an intervention—or choosing to forgo one. Examples of evidence-based messaging scripts are available at the **Reader Resource** web page. But this is so important, that we dedicate an entire section to **Decision Aids** shortly.

3. **Action aids**: Informational pieces that aren't centered around a decision, but which provide directive information for steps to help patients take action. (Silly story to come.)

Action aid story: So one fine day, Sheri has a little health care problem. And it is new. So as a patient she has zero experience with this one. She awakes one morning to discover that her hand is tingling. She heads in to the doctor, who, after administering several tests, hands Sheri a prescription. Sheri now heads out to the nearest pharmacy and hands them the prescription. "What is this?" the pharmacist asks in befuddlement. A colleague looks on with a furrowed brow.

Sheri's brows pull up in response, "A prescription???" she states in uncertainty.

The pharmacist hands the script back to her. "We don't know what this is."

Sheri looks down at the paper. (The writing is very hard to read.) "I think," she says, "it says splint?"

They all look down at the slip of paper. Collectively, heads nod. One of the pharmacists comes out of the pharmacy and leads Sheri to an aisle where they have—well—splints. "Here you go," the pharmacist says, leaving her with a multitude of choices.

And Sheri, having no experience with this, has not a clue what to do.

So just as a decision aid helps a patient make a decision, an action aid actually helps a patient take an action. Sheri needed clarity of action in order to understand that the prescription was a splint for carpal tunnel syndrome and what to do to accomplish this, which required that the people working at the pharmacy be given greater clarity too.

Communications With Patients: Guidance in Brief

We will start with patient communication tools generally. Again, downloadable resources on this section are available at the **Reader Resource** page.

We advise that you first survey the considerations listed at our document, "**Help for Creating Patient Communication Tools**." This idea-generating checklist will give you key considerations for constructing or evaluating patient communication tools.

In brief, we recommend that you consider patient care goals from the Institute of Medicine (IOM) for care that is safe, effective, patient-centered, timely, efficient, equitable [IOM 2001] along with information that is scientifically reliable and quantified information about choices or, in lieu of, transparently tagged information of import to them (e.g., benefits, harms, costs, risks, uncertainties and alternatives including doing nothing).

Our comprehensive tool will give you more considerations such as a checklist for key interventional components (e.g, is this about a diagnosis, treatment, maintenance, etc.?); what are important clinical outcomes for patients (e.g., morbidity, mortality, function, symptom relief, health-related quality of life); suggestions for communication modes (e.g., tone, framing, visual, etc.), media and access; choices for decision-making styles, and more. We do not wish to overstate potential help from the tool—it is merely a checklist—but it can serve you as a set of important things to consider.

Another link available at the **Reader Resource** web page is to our "messaging scripts." A little story. One day we were training a group of clinical pharmacists whose roles were to provide help for patients in long-term care facilities. They told us that they could only communicate with patients' physicians through the patients' charts. Was there some way that we could help them do some evidence-based communications?

So we thought about it and came up with our evidence-based "messaging scripts." Our goals were to create something that was—

1. **Concise**, text table-based;

2. **Patient-centered** and **customizable** to individual patient, caretaker or clinician;

3. **Evidence-based** with short evidence statements, plus key references;

4. **Informative** and **quantitative**;

   - Presents quantified information on baseline risk, benefits and harms in natural language and in ways research suggests may be most easily understood; and,

   - Informs about the benefits and harms of relevant choices, including no treatment.

5. **Flexible**—can add prescribing info, cost info, patient preferences, value considerations, action steps, etc. to customize to topic and need; and,

6. **Utility** oriented;

   - Helps prepare for prepare for communication of health care information using various media.

They were delighted, and you can see samples from a link at the **Reader Resource** web page. Much to our surprise (though maybe it shouldn't have been), we did an evidence-based training program for a group of physicians right after. More on a whim than anything else, we showed them the scripts. They loved them. We subsequently built an entire clinician/patient communication program around them.

Because communications with patients is such a chief concern of ours, we will say a few more things about this. At the **Reader Resource** web page, we also provide a link to a very important tool that has been used as a training tool for doctor/patient communications throughout multiple states that are part of a western coalition via the University of Washington. This is our **GLIDE** tool, standing for "**Greeting, Listen, Inquire & Exchange Information, Determine & Decide and End Encounter**" (gracefully, we might add).

We also have a book available directed to patients that might be of help to you.

What You Don't Know Can Hurt You
A Guide for Patients

Help for Navigating Medical Information & Making Informed Decisions

---

Here's another story about communicating with patients—this example stemming from our evidence messaging scripts. At the health system to which we presented these during a training program, the best clinician communication kudos from attendees went to a nurse who modeled sitting down with a patient and reviewing the script together. She didn't know the evidence on the case example—the script was designed for both clinicians and patients—doing it this way put both her and her patient "**on the same page**," if you will. Both the evidence and the way it was conveyed worked for both the clinician and the patient. If you can achieve this, this is the ideal.

Phase 8. Implementation—Create, Support and Sustain Change

Successful implementation of clinical improvements requires the use of innovative implementation strategies. It has been said that evidence can be thought about as being fairly universal, but "implementation is local." We believe that a checklist representing a set of categories is useful, but that the actual strategies will vary greatly from location to location, depending upon many variables such as local culture, historical considerations, type of organization, etc. The important point is that successful implementation usually results from **applying as many combinations** of the following considerations as possible:

1. Leadership buy-in & support;

2. Decision support materials for clinicians and other target groups;

3. Information dissemination & training;

4. Continuing education and other educational events;

5. Academic detailing (academic detailing is a carefully planned visit to a clinician's office during which a physician or other respected health care professional provides specific valid educational information on a clinical topic);

6. Systems and administrative changes;

7. Patient-centered strategies; and,

8. Measurement & feedback

Example: Implementation strategies utilized by KPHI in the chronic kidney disease guideline mentioned above included the following (**reminder, this is used here only as a past example and should not be assumed to be up-to-date information**):

- Decision Support: Examples of the 1-page algorithm and decision support for patients can be found at the **Reader Resource** web page.

- The guideline recommendations were integrated into a Panel Support Tool, a KPHI proprietary decision-support tool which flags actions that need to be taken on the primary care teams' panels of patients. An example of such a flagged recommendation is "Screen urine microalbumin/creatinine or protein/creatinine annually if glomerular filtration rate (GFR) < 60."

- Large and small group educational events with special sessions devoted to the CKD guidelines were presented—examples include Grand Rounds and other programs using existing forums and standing meetings.

- Renal Population Management: At KPHI, over 80 percent of patients with CKD were managed exclusively in the primary care setting. An innovative system of specialist-directed population management was developed at KPHI. Lab and demographic data were organized, stratified and analyzed by a nephrologist who generates "e-consults," or proactive advice on individual patients at risk, to send to primary care physicians. Such advice included not only recommendations to refer patients with high risk CKD, but also curbside advice to assist primary care physicians in managing their patients with low-moderate risk CKD. The advice included optimizing angiotensin inhibitor drug use, identification of patients not achieving goals for anemia, blood pressure and bone disease, avoiding the use of nephrotoxic medications or special attention to medications that require adjustment. Integrating the evidence-based guidelines into Renal Population Management facilitated consistent, up-to-date recommendations and promoted acceptance of the advice by primary care clinicians.

Phase 9. Measure and Report

Evaluating the success of implementation requires a measurement plan, i.e., a plan that assesses movement toward success in reaching optimal performance as defined by the best available scientific evidence. You measure indicators (e.g., intermediate outcome measures such as lab values, number of prescriptions, etc.) that provide you with information about **changes you have planned and implemented**.

Measuring changes associated with implementing clinical quality improvement activities entails the use of such resources as health records and organizational databases to assess anticipated positive and negative outcomes. You may wish to compare various groups within your organization or your group to outside benchmarks. These measures involve intermediate markers such as measurements of knowledge, changes in the use of various services (e.g., laboratory, imaging, procedures, referrals or other intermediate markers), medications, satisfaction and cost.

Unfortunately, if you are trying to assess health care outcomes using performance measures, the measured outcomes may or may not have resulted from the clinical improvement activity. We say "may or may not" because quality improvement measurements are almost always observational data derived from the health record and databases and are, thus, prone to multiple biases.

Therefore, we repeat an important caution we issued earlier (our glaucoma case example) about the use of databases to assess outcomes—don't try to use your databases to prove that a treatment "works or doesn't work." Recall that for cause-effect associations between interventions and the five clinically important outcomes (morbidity, mortality, symptom relief, functioning and health-related quality of life), valid RCT data are required.

The aim should be to measure such things as the impacts of change on services and patient care—not the five key clinical outcomes.

For these kinds of measures, database information can provide useful before/after information about changes in the care we provide—for example, the number of people in a specific population who have received a guideline-recommended diagnostic or therapeutic intervention (e.g., a lab test, an immunization, etc.). Therefore, use your databases to assess success of implementation.

When conducting measurements of implementation efforts, it is important to think in terms of numerators, denominators and frequencies. For example, a common measurement in CQI work is the hemoglobin A1c test in diabetic patients. For this measurement, the denominator is the population who ought to have had the recommended measurement (diabetics). (Therefore, it is important to carefully define "diabetic" through inclusion and exclusion criteria.) The numerator is the count of the patients in the denominator who received the hemoglobin A1c test. The frequency is the interval between measurements, e.g., the frequency of hemoglobin A1c testing.

The KPHI Chronic Kidney Disease (CKD) project provides a more detailed example of a measurement plan. The following were considered as candidates for the measurement plan (**reminder, this is simply used here as an example, and should not be assumed to be up-to-date information**):

- Rate of achievement of proteinuria goal (Urine protein/creatinine ratio < 1.0);

- Rate of achievement of blood pressure goal (< 130/80);

- Rate of late referrals to Nephrology;

- Rate of referrals to the Anemia Management Service;

- Use of medications to be avoided in CKD; and,

- Clinician satisfaction.

Soon after implementation, KPHI felt comfortable—even though this was not RCT data—in concluding that they had achieved improvements in care of CKD patients. Details have been published by Lee and Forbes [Lee]. Briefly, KPHI experienced a decrease in rate of late referrals and increase in arterio-venous fistula (AVF) rate, an increase in outpatient/inpatient AVF starts, decreased end stage renal disease (ESRD) rate and a decrease in ESRD prevalence. Also there was an increase in urine protein testing (adults not yet on dialysis with a GFR under 60 ml/min within the last 2 years).

Phase 10. Update and Improve

In most cases, the EBCQI team leader or other individual must stay involved with the project in order for it to continue successfully. Someone—usually a clinical team member—should accept responsibility for monitoring key evidence changes in the medical literature and periodically formally updating the guideline. Updates are recommended when important evidence or significant new information becomes available and, formally, in our opinion, every 2 years. Thus, a process of continual monitoring is important. Updating requires conducting literature searches and evidence reviews as described earlier.

Example: Our department, the Department of Clinical Improvement and Education, at Group Health Cooperative in Seattle, was responsible for updating many clinical guidelines. Staff in the department were skilled in carrying out the evidence-based CQI activities described in this book (emphasis on evidence). They—together with our librarians—conducted searches of the medical literature and updated the multiple guidelines, providing the critically-appraised evidence along with support to the EBCQI teams who would meet and update the clinical guidelines at the guideline expiration date or if important new information became available. If guidelines were not updated, they were retired.

Summary—Key Requirements for The Optimally Functioning EBCQI Team

In this book, we have described the 5 core requirements (1. support, knowledge and effectiveness through leadership; 2. committed culture to evidence-based patient-centered care; 3. true evidence-based approach; 4. correct and supportive work components; and, 5. skilled, engaged individuals in needed roles) + 10 process steps for successfully and efficiently creating EBCQI projects which can improve health care outcomes for patients and achieve other improvement goals:

> Phase 1. Organizational Readiness
> Phase 2. Clinical Improvement Project & Team Selection
> Phase 3. Project Preparation & Outline
> Phase 4. Evidence Identification, Selection & Review
> Phase 5. Clinical Content Development
> Phase 6. Impact Assessment
> Phase 7. Communication Tools Development
> Phase 8. Implementation—Create, Support and Sustain Change
> Phase 9. Measure and Report
> Phase 10. Update and Improve

Each of these steps contribute to effective clinical improvement—to a final set of proposed changes and accompanying materials, which, if successfully implemented, can improve outcomes and the use of resources.

Every successful EBCQI team will have the support of local leadership. They will have needed skills, resources and time. They will be supported by efficient group processes, effective and efficient work components and tools. The project will have a "champion" who will lead the improvement and, with the help of others, ensure successful project management and implementation along with sustainability.

Members must be engaged and knowledgeable about their roles which will frequently require just-in-time training. *Ad hoc* team members may be required if the team is not skilled at key evidence-based tasks such as searching and critical appraisal of the medical literature. Meetings must be conducted efficiently and documented. Transparent, evidence-based processes using various tools and templates to prepare materials, summarize evidence, create, implement, measure and update clinical improvements are required. Below we list some of these key requirements:

1. **Leadership support, cultural receptivity** and **effective project support**;

2. Correct and effective **evidence-based approach** which includes effective **documentation and transparent processes**;

3. Correct **work components** which include systematic **strategies and methods** to obtain, filter, synthesize and update decision-support materials with **relevant evidence** and **tools** to assist in critical appraisal, synthesis and translation of the evidence into usable documents that fit organizational needs and requirements;

4. Optimal processes for **project selection, team and leader selection** and for **conducting meetings**;

5. Engaged, effective **team leaders and members** in needed roles with effective skills including—

   • Understanding **critical appraisal principles, concepts, approaches, methods and tools** and the members' role in triangulating evidence with other considerations to create final products and recommendations;

   • **Critical appraisal skills** or assistance from others with critical appraisal skills to evaluate the evidence;

   • **Economic** and other **impact analysis skills**;

6. Creation of effective **clinical content** and **communication aids** such as decision-support materials;

7. **Communication of information and facilitation of appropriate decisions and actions** which will result in optimal outcomes for patients;

8. Effective mechanisms for **creating, implementing, supporting and sustaining change**;

9. Effective **measurement methods** and **reporting** mechanisms; and,

10. Mechanisms for keeping **up-to-date** and **improving—or at times, retiring**—the improvement.

CONCLUSION

Evidence-based clinical quality improvement—when appropriately applied—is a foundational activity with effective processes for providing high quality and value-based patient care.

The evidence-based approach to informing clinical quality improvements is powerful because it provides a solid, scientific basis and the tools for making judgments about the validity and clinical usefulness of interventions. An evidence-based approach builds on appropriate study design, methodology, execution and good study performance outcomes, and it considers the weight of the resulting scientific evidence to identify gaps in clinical care, inform decisions and provide the power—due to evidence-based rationale—to drive clinical practice change and improve outcomes for patients.

The evidence-based approach is critical for determining overall benefits, risks, therapeutic alternatives, uncertainties, patient and provider satisfaction, costs and other considerations so that EBCQI members can make appropriate choices about interventions.

Using our Kaiser Permanente Hawaii VTE project as an example, important keys to success included—

1. Committed and knowledgeable **leadership**;

2. Good project **selection** with the right scope and careful crafting of key clinical questions;

3. **Resources and time**;

4. **Person-power**—and **outstanding team**;

5. Attention to the uniqueness of **culture** and other **local issues**;

6. Applying the correct **process steps**;

7. **Skills** including in effective leadership, clinical knowledge, EBCQI processes, with emphasis on evidence-based skills;

8. Seed **sources** and **evidence**; and,

9. Planning **efficiency strategies** including **tools and templates**.

In the words of Karen Ching MD, project leader, "This project was an important investment to our institution. At the most fundamental level, the project encourages evidence-based practice and thinking. For the hospital, it means a focus on quality and patient-related outcomes."

READER RESOURCE WEB PAGE

For tools and online resources:

http://www.delfinigrouppublishing.com/EBCQI-resources.html

APPENDICES

Appendix A: Sample Critical Appraisal

Appendix B: Interview Questions to Help You Determine Evidence-Based Know-How and Sophistication

APPENDIX A: Sample Critical Appraisal

Below we provide you with what a critical appraisal might look like. There is no one way to do this—so you might devise another method completely. We have another example at a link at the **Reader Resource** web page. In this instance we have elected to use our short critical appraisal checklist to provide examples of critical appraisal considerations. Often we top something like this with an abstract from the study, with occasional (rare) annotations from us if we think that the abstract is missing something major such as safety results.

So for this sample, pretend that you have just finished reading an abstract of an imaginary study immediately before the appraisal sample.

~ Imaginary Abstract ~

Appraisal

Reference (include PMID number):

Appraisor(s):

Date of Appraisal:

General: Note sponsorship, funding and affiliations, recognizing that any entity or person involved in research may have a bias.

Notes: NIH Grant, university directed study

Study Design Assessment	☐ **Is the design appropriate to the research question? Is the research question useful?**
	☐ For **efficacy**, use of **experimental study design** (meaning there was no choice made to determine intervention)
	☐ **Clinically significant area** for study (morbidity, mortality, symptom relief, functioning and health-related quality of life) and reasonable **definitions for clinical outcome such as response, treatment success or failure**

	☐ If **composite endpoints** used, reasonable combination used.
	☐ Ensure **prespecified** and **appropriate** 1) research questions, 2) populations to analyze, and 3) outcomes
Study Design Risk of Bias Rating: Low	**Bias Assessment** • No biases identified considering items above. **Notes** •

Internal Validity Assessment: Can bias, confounding or chance explain the study results? See below

Selection Bias	☐ Groups are **appropriate** for study, of appropriate size, **concurrent** and **similar** in **prognostic variables** ☐ Methods for generating the group assignment sequence are truly **random,** sequencing avoids potential for anyone **affecting assignment** to a study arm and **randomization remains intact** ☐ **Concealment of allocation** strategies are employed to prevent anyone affecting assignment to a study arm
Selection Risk of Bias Rating: Medium	**Bias Assessment** • Title says randomized; however, no details of randomization provided. Baseline characteristics appear balanced between groups, suggestive that randomization was performed successfully. • No other biases identified considering items above. **Notes**

	• Allocation to treatment groups was concealed through use of a call-in center. However, it is not known if the center staff had a random method for allocation.
Performance Bias	☐ **Double-blinding** methods employed (i.e., subject and all working with the subject or subject's data) and achieved ☐ Reasonable **intervention** and reasonable **comparator** used (e.g., placebo) ☐ **No bias or difference, except for what is under study, between groups during course of study** (e.g., intervention design and execution, care experiences, co-interventions, concomitant medication use, adherence, inappropriate exposure or migration, cross-over threats, protocol deviations, study duration, changes due to time etc.)
Performance Risk of Bias Rating: **Low, but see Assessment**	**Bias Assessment** • No biases identified considering items above (however, uncertainty about blinded assessment—see Assessment). **Notes** • A review of side effects shows a reasonable enough balance between groups and so unlikely to become unblinded due to side effects.
Data/Attrition Bias	☐ Evaluate bias in **measurement activities** ☐ Might **attrition**, including missing data, discontinuations or loss to follow-up, have resulted in distorted outcomes?
Data/Attrition Risk of Bias Rating: **Medium**	**Bias Assessment** • No biases identified considering items above; however, see below.

	Notes
	• Discontinuations were high at 30 percent. Despite this high attrition, however, attrition bias seems unlikely.
	○ Randomization was likely to have been achieved, concealment of allocation method was appropriate, blinding at least before assessment appears likely to have been successful, high adherence, low protocol violations, groups were not treated differently except for the intervention, co-interventions were balanced between groups, reasons for discontinuations were balanced between groups (6 categories listed), data imputation was appropriate, and patterns in outcomes make chance unlikely.
	○ Given the above, it seems unlikely that a significant number of discontinued people in the comparator group would have had good outcomes, had they completed the study, in sufficient numbers to reverse the results or render statistically significant findings non-significant.
Assessment Bias & Chance Assessment	☐ Assessors are **blinded** ☐ Low likelihood of findings due to **chance, false positive and false negative outcomes** ☐ **Non-significant findings** are reported, but the **confidence intervals include clinically meaningful differences** ☐ **Intention-to-Treat Analysis (ITT)** performed for efficacy (**not safety**) (all people are analyzed as randomized + reasonable

	method for imputing missing values which puts the intervention through a challenging trial or reasonable sensitivity analysis) or missing values are very small. ☐ If **time-to-event analysis** performed, appropriate, transparent and unbiased. Evaluate **censoring** rules. ☐ **Analysis methods** are appropriate and use of **modeling** only with use of reasonable assumptions ☐ No problems of **selective reporting or selective exclusion of outcomes**
Assessment Risk of Bias Rating: **Uncertain due to assessment blinding; otherwise low** **Risk of Chance Results: Low**	**Bias Assessment** • No specific mention of blinded assessment or that all working with subjects' data were blinded. • Non-significance in primary outcome of all-cause mortality is probably due to lack of power for that outcome (i.e., rare event may mean that too few people were studied to show a true difference)—that the problem may be a power issue is supported by the confidence intervals which include a clinically meaningful difference. This is also supported by a pattern of statistical significance in the individual outcomes (all pre-specified) of reduction in new onset of heart failure, reduction in non-fatal myocardial infarction plus reduction in hospital admissions for myocardial infarction or heart failure. • No other biases identified considering items above. **Notes** • Efficacy analysis was by intention-to-treat (all subjects by groups). Mixed effects model is appropriate for data

	imputation.
	• All key outcomes reported, so appears to be no problems with selective reporting.
	• Patterns in outcomes make chance unlikely.

Usefulness & Other Considerations	
Meaningful Clinical Benefit	☐ Clinically significant **area** + sufficient benefit **size** = meaningful clinical benefit (consider efficacy vs effectiveness)
	☐ **Safety** (caution re: new interventions, caution re: non-significant findings)
Efficacy Evaluation **Safety Evaluation**	**Efficacy Results Assessment** • Clinically significant areas with clinically meaningful effect sizes. If the study had been conducted with more people, reduction in mortality is likely. **Safety Assessment** • Population was appropriate for safety (patients not as randomized, but as actually treated provided they had at least one exposure to the study drug). • No significant safety issues reported.
Overall Grade and Summary	**Grade B to BU** **Summary** • Results are clinically meaningful and likely to be true. Confirmatory studies desirable.

APPENDIX B: Interview Questions to Help You Determine Evidence-Based Know-How and Sophistication (Taken From Our Pharmacy & Therapeutics Handbook)

In this section, we give you a choice of questions that you can pose to candidates for your evidence-based information gathering and evaluation tasks, whether they be people you are considering hiring or individuals representing companies from whom you are considering acquiring information.

In creating this list, we have cherry-picked some items that we think are good choices for a little biopsy of a person's evidence-based knowledge and which are likely to be reasonably readily understood by you regardless of your evidence-based expertise. (It's a little bit like going to a foreign country, armed with a few words of the native tongue and asking the question, "Where is the nearest bank?" You are likely to receive a barrage of sound that is completely unintelligible to you. And may not get you to the bank! So while we, ourselves, might choose entirely different questions if we were taking on such an assessment task, we think these questions can provide some utility to those who are not as familiar with critical appraisal as we are.)

First we will present you with the "flavor" of our questions, to give you a general idea, which we will follow by elaborating on the exact phrasing of our suggested questions along with details for how you might evaluate a response. You may want to select from these rather than use them all; however, you might want to keep to this order since changing the sequence may, at times, give away the store. Further, we've attempted to craft these questions very carefully—a change in wording could radically change what might be an appropriate answer.

1. **Observations**: Do you think that well-done database research and *post-hoc* analyses of study data can provide us with useful evidence about the efficacy of interventions?"

2. **Searching**: How do you determine which studies to include in a monograph to answer efficacy questions? How do you ensure that your search includes MeSH terms?

3. **Acquiring**: In considering questions of efficacy, how might you use an abstract?

4. **Appraising**: What is your approach to reading a medical research study? (This is one of our favorites.) Many more appraising questions including...

5. What makes for an appropriate comparison group?

6. Discuss blinding.

7. How do you define intention-to-treat (ITT) analysis? How would you evaluate an intention-to-treat analysis?

8. How do you approach the issue of people unable to complete the study?

9. What is your approach to evaluating censoring in time-to-event (TTE) analyses?

10. **Evaluating Outcomes**: How do you know if a trial was adequately powered? (Commonly not understood, FYI.) And several more questions, including—

11. What is your approach to evaluating clinical significance?

12. Describe the difference between absolute and relative differences in reported outcomes?

13. How might confidence intervals be used to assess the results of a study?

14. **Secondary Sources**: How do you evaluate them?

Interview Questions—Specific Questions & Answer Ideals

Questions: Database Research or Real World Data (Observations)

Question 1: "Do you think that well-done database research and *post-hoc* analyses of study data can provide us with useful evidence about the efficacy of interventions?"

Answer Advice

A "yes" answer means that this respondent may be relying on highly misleading medical science. The important thing to find out is whether the respondent understands the difference between experimental and observational evidence and the role of observational evidence. If the respondent believes, for example, that database studies can prove that an intervention "works," he or she does not understand the difference between experiments and observations—and does not understand that observations (with the rare exception of all-or-none results) can be misleading when trying to determine the efficacy of an intervention which is a cause and effect question.

Examples of appropriate use of observational data include identification of populations of interest; evaluation of the success of implementation of changes; identifying variation in practice; performing limited extensions of clinical trials (e.g., for safety); evaluating adherence; economic projections; and, more. But not for determine cause and effect (excluding our rare exception). Safety too, is a cause and effect question—but, as we have already described—at times, observational data is used for safety and at a price of being potentially misleading.

Question 2a: Systematic Searching

"If I were to ask you to conduct an evidence review for the **efficacy** of a drug that has been on the market for several years, how would you determine what research studies to include in the review?" (Note: It is important that you emphasize efficacy because safety or another clinical question might invite an entirely different approach.)

Answer Advice

At a minimum, a good response should include the performance of a **systematic search** utilizing the **National Library of Medicine (NLM)**. **PubMed**® is the user interface for searching—so if their answer includes either, that is good. A systematic search means that they are going to apply a process for casting a wide net to identify potentially relevant studies.

For efficiency, they should know that they can apply appropriate **"limits" and exclusions** to narrow their search. For questions of efficacy, it is reasonable to limit their search for clinical trials—and even to limit those to only those using randomization or minimization. (Minimization is a non-random study group allocation process which even sophisticated evidence evaluators may not know about. We mention it here because if they tell you they would include studies using minimization, that is fine. If they say nothing about minimization, that too, is fine. For simplicity's sake, understand that our comments about RCTs generally pertain to studies using minimization too.)

Relying upon randomization or minimization is likely to result in balanced groups for study, which is vitally important. Here an example of appropriate exclusion criteria:

> "We excluded studies not published in the English language, studies not relevant to the question, animal studies, editorials,

opinion pieces, abstracts without full documentation of research, narrative reviews, observational studies for determining efficacy of interventions, studies deemed to be fatally flawed from bias and studies not useful for answering key clinical questions."

Another acceptable approach is to search for systematic reviews—meaning secondary studies that utilize formal methods for combining studies. Ideally, we find a high quality systematic review that only utilizes reliable primary studies which have passed a rigorous critical appraisal. If the systematic review is flawed because of the inclusion of studies that are not valid, we evaluate it to determine if the authors have done an effective job of searching and excluding studies that we would, ourselves, be likely to exclude. If yes, then we can rely upon their study yield. We then critically appraise their included studies (you may just wish to sample them, although we think this is risky), updating to include new valid RCTs since the search date. This is often a huge time-saver when we are lucky enough to find such a review.

Question 2b: MeSH Terms

"How do you ensure that your search includes MeSH terms?"

Answer Advice

MeSH stands for Medical Subject Headings which is a list of synonyms or thesaurus of terms used by search databases to index and classify medical information. After entering their search terms, they should check PubMed's **"Search details"** to see if MeSH terms were applied. Example: Including the word "diabetic" in a PubMed search will not result in the application of a MeSH term, but "diabetes" will and, therefore, will yield more studies. If they do not do this confirmation, and adjust their search as needed, they might miss important studies.

Question 3: Abstracts

"In considering questions of efficacy, how might you use an abstract?"

Answer Advice

If they say that they do not use study abstracts, that is fine. If they say they use them to isolate key pieces of information, that is fine—but only if they indicate that they would not use information from abstracts of studies that have not been critically appraised and determined to be valid.

You cannot determine whether a study is reliable from the abstract. However, it can be useful for ruling studies out on the basis of relevancy or sometimes because a lethal threat to validity might stand out. It can also be useful for ruling in studies for further critical appraisal. And when it comes to efficacy questions, that is it!

Questions: Critical Appraisal of Primary Studies

Reminder: We are not giving you comprehensive questions—only a select few. Also, preceding these questions, you should explain that you are asking for answers in the context of "**questions of efficacy in studies reporting superiority of interventions**."

Question 4: Critically Appraising

"When considering efficacy, once you acquire the full text of a clinical trial, what do you do with it?" or, if you want to use colloquial lingo, "What is your approach to reading a study when considering efficacy?"

Answer Advice

Candidates should tell you that they **critically appraise** it. If they stop at that point, you then want to probe deeper to get a sense of how they approach critical appraisal. A good answer will indicate that they are not just "reading the study," but are using some formal **process** which includes **criteria**.

A best answer will indicate that they demonstrate the importance of experiments—not observations—when assessing a study involving therapy, prevention or screening) and are looking for the **effects of bias and chance on study results**. They may mention specific types of bias such as selection, performance, measurement, attrition and assessment bias—if they do so, this is an indicator of knowledge. If they only indicate that they are interested in statistical methods and do not mention bias, they **do not** understand critical appraisal.

Sheri's broad criteria is essentially question number 1 with a sideline trip at times using question number 2, such as in the case of a valid study with a high degree of attrition:

1) **Can anything explain the results other than truth**?

2) What conditions would need to be present if the results are not true?

To assess this, she looks for the presence of bias and chance by evaluating a series of elements such as randomization, allocation of patients to study groups, blinding, differences between groups, adherence, measurement, attrition, analysis methods and so on, using—but not limiting herself to—a set of formal criteria. More sophisticated evidence evaluators often use a formal **checklist** to help ensure they are not overlooking items for consideration, understanding that applying critical thinking and considering the contextual elements of a study is crucial.

At the **Reader Resource** web page, we make available several critical appraisal tools to help you with this work.

Question 5: Creating Equal Groups

First a backgrounder in case this is helpful. Equal groups are REQUIRED for studying the efficacy of interventions. Randomization (and potentially "minimization" which we are not going to further describe) are the ONLY ways to balance the prognostic variables between groups. And even then, random chance might mess with the distribution—which is why a review of the table of baseline characteristics can be helpful to see if randomization was likely to be successful.

There can be NO difference between groups for study—excluding what is being studied, i.e., drug versus placebo. ANY difference between groups except for that is automatically a bias and may be the cause of, explain or distort results. So an understanding of this is a requirement.

Question 5a: Equal Groups vs "Comparison Group" Disguising A Case Series

Do you consider historical controls or statistical averages of disease outcomes to be appropriate comparisons when evaluating the efficacy of an intervention?

Answer Advice

Setting aside our all-or-none instances, a "yes" answer means that this person may be relying on highly misleading medical science.

Question 5b: Equal Groups vs Observational Studies

"Can you explain any "issues" with the following statement: "A study comparing women who chose to take antioxidants daily, with those who did not, has demonstrated that antioxidants protect against heart disease.""

Answer Advice

The above example is from an "observational study." A good answer will explain that cause and effect cannot be concluded from observational studies with the rare exception of all-or-none results—if any claims can be made, it should only be that there is an association. (Not all associations are cause and effect.)

Question 5c: Equal Groups vs Magically Making Them Equal

"Do you agree that, if care is taken to match subjects with controls on key prognostic variables through methods such as adjustment or propensity scoring, then matching is likely to be effective in preventing selection bias?"

Answer Advice

The appropriate answer is **no**. You cannot create equal groups for study through statistical adjustments. Processes that are best likely to result in balanced groups are randomization and minimization. (Note: No points lost if candidates have never heard about, nor understand minimization.)

Question 6: Blinding

Inadequate blinding has been shown to distort study results up to a relative 72 percent [Juni, Kjaergard, Moher, Savovic, Schulz] and may even distort results of hard outcomes such as mortality [example Marciniak].

Question 6a: Blinding Success

How do you evaluate blinding?

Answer Advice

A good answer to this question should address the following—

1. A recognition that details need to be provided—meaning, that it is insufficient to see the term "double-blinded" in the article without specifics of how blinding was achieved. This includes such things as pills that look and taste the same; double-dummy design so that if a comparison is made between an active agent in pill form and one in injection form, each patient also gets a placebo version which masks the mode of administration; and so forth.

2. An awareness that the subject and everyone who comes into contact with the subject or his or her data do not know the treatment assignment. This includes blinded assessment.

3. An attempt to think through whether success of blinding was likely. Firstly, researchers should not "test" the guesses of their subjects or others involved in the research such as subjects' physicians or evaluators. If they do and everybody guesses wrong, fine. But if they guessed "correctly," this doesn't mean the blind has been broken either, but may be a result of chance or pre-trial hunches about efficacy [Sackett]. Rather, optimally interviewees raise this issue and then discuss that they would look to clues within the trial itself such as unblinding due to a blood test or a review of safety outcomes to see if a blind may have been broken due to an excessive number of people presenting with a particular adverse event.

4. Bonus if they state that the assignment of people to their study groups should be hidden (such as through the use of a call center).

The technical term for this is "concealment of allocation." Not raising this should not result in a penalty to the interviewee as the term "blinding," in the evidence-based culture, is reserved for what happens after allocation to study groups. However, a person who raises this issue is demonstrating some true skill in critical appraisal.

Question 6b: Blinding vs Outcomes

For which outcomes is blinding important? Self-reported pain? Physician-assessed improvement in function? Tumor progression or remission? Death?

Answer Advice

All of them. Many people think that blinding is only important for soft or subjective outcomes and not objective or hard outcomes, such as death. This is not true. Sometimes when we teach critical appraisal to a group of physicians, we say, "Raise your hand if you think you can affect the life or death of a patient." They ALL raise their hands. Thus, blinding is important in hard outcomes as well.

A good case in point is the RECORD trial in which participating physicians were not blinded, but adjudicating outcome assessors were [Marciniak, Psaty]. This resulted in a bias in which fewer deaths were sent for review to the outcome assessors by physicians, underestimating risk of death from rosiglitazone.

Question 6c: Blinding and Then, Unblinding

"How would you utilize results from an otherwise valid study that is successfully double-blinded for 12 weeks and then continues as an open-label trial for an additional 12 weeks?"

Answer Advice

You want to learn what weight they give to the **importance of blinding**. The ideal answer would be that candidates would **utilize only blinded data for**

efficacy. If they state they would evaluate subsequent data for safety and potentially other considerations such as adherence, that is fine—however, they should include a caveat that this information, too, may be affected by lack of blinding.

For the next two questions, we are providing you with a **combined answer.**

Question 7a: Definition of Intention-to-treat (ITT) Analysis

How would you define intention-to-treat (ITT) analysis?

Question 7b: Evaluation of Intention-to-treat (ITT) Analyses

How would you evaluate an intention-to-treat analysis?

Combined Answer Advice

Your first goal is to gain an understanding as to whether your candidates know what this is. As we described earlier, for dichotomous outcomes of efficacy in superiority trials, ITT analysis is historically considered by many experts to be a favored analysis method. ITT analysis requires that patients are analyzed in the group to which they are randomized regardless of the actual intervention received and regardless of study completion or completeness of data, which requires the use of some reasonable method for assigning missing data points (data imputation).

To recap this in brief, "As randomized, so analyzed."

Your candidates should demonstrate an understanding of these points. To summarize—

1. ITT analysis should be the primary population analysis method for **dichotomous efficacy outcomes**. Not for safety, which should be as treated.

2. All patients must be **analyzed** by the group to which they were **randomized**.

3. **Data are included for all subjects**, requiring some method to impute data if outcomes information is missing.

4. **Imputation methods must be evaluated** to determine whether they seem reasonable or not.

5. If ITT analysis was not done, then h**ow much data are missing, and is it likely that missing data are likely to have distorted results?** If not, then lack of ITT analysis may be a minor issue.

There are two frequently used approaches for imputing missing data. The first method attempts to **estimate "truth."** The second method attempts to pose a challenge by **setting a higher bar for reaching statistical significance**. Typically, even more experienced evidence reviewers will be inexperienced when it comes to evaluating imputed data. However, this evaluation is important because—as you can imagine—choices that are made can have very meaningful effects on reported outcomes.

The more sophisticated evidence reviewers will 1) be aware that **last-observation-carried forward or LOCF** is prone to bias, but under certain ideal circumstances may have some utility (although this last point is rarely known and so should carry no penalty); 2) know that **mixed effects models** are preferable for guestimating "truth" as compared to LOCF; and, 3) understand that raising the bar for **statistical testing** can be useful in many instances. They may even have skills and experience in performing their own ITT analyses to be able to reanalyze data from otherwise valid studies.

> **Important Note 1**: Repeat—ITT analysis is not appropriate for analyzing safety outcomes because it could mask important safety information.

> **Important Note 2**: ITT is not appropriate for the primary analysis in non-inferiority and equivalence trials if the data imputation methods favor no difference between groups, which is often the case.

Question 8: Attrition + Attrition Bias

"How do you approach the issue of people unable to complete the study?"

Answer Advice

This is a tricky area, and so this is a more subtle consideration. But it is important because, for many indications, people will not be able to complete the trial— in oncology trials, for example.

Research has not provided much understanding about the potential distortion of results from discontinuation. We have seen radical changes in the p-value based on a small differential between groups at 4.4 percent. Some journals will not publish studies with 20 percent attrition or more. On the other hand, we have evaluated studies where 50 percent or more of study subjects were unable to complete the trial, and we rated the study to be of high quality with improbable bias from attrition.

This is a classic example of "it depends." Our approach is to look at all elements of what otherwise makes for a valid study and then consider what would be required for the results not to be true. For example, imagine that a study is strong in terms of likely success of blinding, continued balanced groups, high adherence rates and no likely effect from confounding treatments. In this case, a high attrition rate might only have the impact of making a smaller sample size (thus posing a greater risk for false non-significant findings), but not otherwise distort the results.

Sheri's favored overarching critical appraisal question number 2 sometimes comes into play here: "What conditions would need to be present if the results are not true?" To evaluate this, when assessing the likelihood of attrition to have resulted in attrition bias, at times, we conduct our own sensitivity analyses to see what it might take to overturn statistical significance and then evaluate the likelihood of this being plausible.

As a hypothetical example, imagine a high quality study, yet with high attrition, comparing two active agents. Let us say that drug A is the winner over drug B. Now imagine that statistical significance could only be overturned if a large number of drug B patients discontinuing their study medication would otherwise have had improved results at a much higher event rate than those drug B patients who actually completed the study, had they been able to complete their course of treatment. Depending upon contextual elements, a scenario like this might be highly implausible and, therefore, attrition would be highly unlikely to have resulted in attrition bias.

Question 9: Time-to-Event (TTE) Analyses

"What is your approach to evaluating censoring in time-to-event analyses?"

Answer Advice

"Censoring" is the practice of no longer including a patient's data in a survival curve. Sophisticated evidence evaluators will know that the censoring of patients **who have not experienced the outcome of interest** by the study's end (also known as "administrative" or "right" censoring) is appropriate.

The risk of distortion of results may be high, however, when patients are removed for other reasons, such as violation of protocols and other reasons determined by the investigators such as a censoring rule stating that death could not be due to drug A if it occurred 14 days after discontinuing the drug.

Experienced evaluators will know that they need to evaluate the **censoring rules** to see if they may be biased in some way. (They will also know that censoring rules are rarely reported, so evaluating censoring rules is often impossible and may result in the study being rated as being of uncertain validity.)

Questions: Evaluating Outcomes

Question 10: Power

"In a study of reduction in mortality using a new agent, if investigators reported that a sample size of 5,000 subjects was assumed adequate to provide a power of 85% or more, how would you know if the study was adequately powered for that outcome?"

Answer Advice

Power means that enough people were studied to find a statistically significant difference, if an actual difference exists. If the outcome was **statistically significant**, it was sufficiently powered. Period.

If the outcome was **not statistically significant**, then it is unknown— either there truly was no statistically significant difference between the groups or the study was not powered (did not have enough subjects) to show a difference if a difference truly exists. Confidence intervals, however, may provide a practical solution to address the questions raised by non-significance if they do not include the potential for meaningful clinical benefit within their range.

An incorrect answer would be to determine how many subject they enrolled or how many subjects completed the study. If their power calculation was for 5,000 people and 10,000 patients completed the trial, if results were non-significant, it could still be the case that the study was "underpowered"— meaning, it could still be possible that they didn't have enough people in the study to show an existing difference. The power calculation is of use for researchers doing subsequent research, but should be ignored by a critical appraiser.

Question 11: Clinical Significance

"What is your approach to evaluating clinical significance?"

Answer Advice

To be clinically useful means that expected outcomes will be of value to a patient. To judge this, there are two primary considerations: firstly, the likelihood of experiencing an overall beneficial outcome (i.e., size of the outcome); and, secondly, whether the outcome is proven to be of benefit in things that matter to patients. This means that the intervention has been proven to be useful to patients in the areas of 1) morbidity; 2) mortality; 3) symptom relief; 4) mental, emotional or physical functioning; or, 5) health-related quality of life. These are things that you can personally experience. These are called "clinical outcomes."

Much medical science targets other types of outcomes for which there may be speculation—but no proof—of benefit in these areas. There are numerous names for this type of outcome such as intermediate outcome, intermediate marker, surrogate marker, proxy marker, etc. They all mean the same thing—in effect, something that stands in for something else. An example would be some change in bone density for which you do not experience any symptoms.

If we have reliable proof that affecting a surrogate marker, such as improving your bone density, will lead to one of the clinical outcomes above, such as reduction in fracture, then the surrogate will qualify as a meaningful outcome. However, often we do not have reliable proof, only speculation which may make "logical sense." And time and time again, speculating about the benefit of non-clinical outcomes has ultimately been proven to be very wrong even when it does make sense—and worse, many patients have come to harm.

At a minimum, candidates' answers should distinguish between **clinically significant outcomes** (e.g., morbidity, mortality, symptom relief, functioning and health-related quality of life) and intermediate or surrogate outcomes (e.g., lab measures such as carotid intima-media thickness) that may or may not be meaningful proxy markers for clinically meaningful outcomes. They should express that intermediate markers require valid proof of achieving a clinical outcome.

Also at a minimum candidates' answers should also address the importance of the **size of the outcomes**. Which leads us to...

Question12: Absolute vs Relative Measures of Outcomes

"Explain the difference between absolute risk reduction and relative risk reduction and, if you had to choose only one to be reported in a clinical trial, which would you choose and why?"

Answer Advice

Absolute risk reduction (ARR) is the **difference** (expressed in percent) in the outcome rates in the two groups. **Relative risk reduction** (RRR) is the **proportional difference** (expressed in percent) in the outcome rates.

Example

Control group: 10 out of 100 improve
Study group: 15 out of 100 improve

In this example, 15 percent minus 10 percent = 5 percent; therefore, the ARR is 5 percent. Ten is one third smaller than 15; one third equals 33 percent. So the RRR is 33 percent.

Relative risk reduction can have its uses for doing risk calculations. However, ARR is preferred over RRR for reporting results of clinical trials. Knowing only the RRR is akin to knowing everything in a store is 90 percent off—and then turning over your credit card without knowing the baseline price. Relative risk reduction can be equal to the ARR, but can never be smaller. Usually it is a lot bigger and so it presents a mathematically accurate answer, but one that tends to emotionally exaggerate the outcomes.

A truly savvy evaluator will tell you that ARR is helpful, but that it, too, may distort decision-making without the raw numbers such as risk with and without treatment, as we described earlier.

Question 13: Use of Confidence Intervals

"In reporting the results of an RCT investigating an anticoagulant for prophylaxis of venous thromboembolism in total knee replacement surgery, investigators report, 'Groups A and B did not differ in clinically relevant bleeding.' How would you check to see if the authors' conclusion about no difference was misleading?"

Answer Advice

The ideal answer will acknowledge that the **confidence intervals** should be evaluated to determine whether they include a potentially clinically meaningful value.

Questions: Evaluating Secondary Studies and Sources

Question 14a: Evaluating Secondary Sources in General

"In considering the efficacy of an intervention, once you acquire a secondary source that may provide recommendations about it—such as a clinical guideline—what do you do with it?"

Answer Advice

No points are lost if the term "secondary source" is not familiar to them. Again, we use the term to refer to any medical information source that utilizes primary or secondary studies. These would include clinical guidelines and recommendations, health care economic studies, compendia, protocols, etc.

Once understood, candidates' answers should include an acknowledgment that the primary and secondary study information **must be critically appraised** whether directly by the candidate or indirectly by someone else. If the secondary source indicates that studies were critically appraised, then candidates should answer that they would need to **evaluate the**

effectiveness of that process and may need to critically appraise the included studies themselves.

Further, there is a difference between the quality of the studies included in a secondary source and the quality of the secondary source itself. Therefore, the quality of the secondary source must also be evaluated.

Sometimes a secondary source is well-done, but valid science is lacking. In this instance, the source should label the strength of the evidence. The source should also include strength-of-recommendation tags for any recommendations it makes.

Use of a valid secondary source should also include awareness of the need to update the source for additional valid science published after the original search date.

Bonus points if the respondent reveals an awareness that most secondary studies and sources are often problematic because they do not provide valid information.

Question 14b: Evaluating Pharmacoeconomic and Other Cost Effectiveness Studies

"Once you acquire a pharmacoeconomic study, how do you evaluate it?"

Answer Advice

Again, candidates' answers should include an acknowledgment that the primary and secondary study information **must be critically appraised** whether directly by the authors or someone else. If the secondary source indicates that studies were critically appraised, then candidates should answer that they would need to **evaluate the effectiveness of that process and may need to critically appraise the included studies themselves**. Frequently, "cost-effectiveness" studies are done with no regard to actually having determined effectiveness which requires that the intervention has proven efficacy!

And again, there is a difference between the quality of the studies included in a secondary source and the quality of the secondary source itself. Therefore, the quality of the health care economic study must also be subjected to critical appraisal.

REFERENCES

1. Abernethy AP, Raman G, Balk EM, Hammond JM, Orlando LA, Wheeler JL, Lau J,McCrory DC. Systematic review: reliability of compendia methods for off-label oncology indications. Ann Intern Med. 2009 Mar 3;150(5):336-43. Epub 2009 Feb 16.Review. Erratum in: Ann Intern Med. 2009 Apr 21;150(8):571. PubMed PMID:19221366. AHRQ Review of Compendia: http://www.ahrq.gov/about/annualconf09/abernethy.htm

2. Atkins D, Chang S, Gartlehner G, Buckley DI, Whitlock EP, Berliner E, Matchar D. Assessing the Applicability of Studies When Comparing Medical Interventions. 2010 Dec 30. Methods Guide for Effectiveness and Comparative Effectiveness Reviews [Internet]. Rockville (MD): Agency for Health care Research and Quality (US); 2008-. Available from http://www.ncbi.nlm.nih.gov/books/NBK53480/ PubMed PMID: 21433409.

3. Beck, A.T., Ward, C. H., Mendelson, M., Mock, J., & Erbaugh, J. (1961) An inventory for measuring depression. Archives of General Psychiatry, 4, 561-571. And Beck, A. T., Steer, R.A., & Garbin, M.G. (1988) Psychometric properties of the Beck Depression Inventory: Twenty-five years of evaluation. Clinical Psychology Review, 8(1), 77-100.

4. Bombardier C, Laine L, Reicin A, Shapiro D, Burgos-Vargas R, Davis B, Day R, Ferraz MB, Hawkey CJ, Hochberg MC, Kvien TK, Schnitzer TJ; VIGOR Study Group. Comparison of upper gastrointestinal toxicity of rofecoxib and naproxen in patients with rheumatoid arthritis. VIGOR Study Group. N Engl J Med. 2000 Nov 23;343(21):1520-8, 2 p following 1528. PubMed PMID: 11087881.

5. Braddick M, Stuart M, Hrachovec J. The use of balance sheets in developing clinical guidelines. J Am Board Fam Pract. 1999 Jan-Feb;12(1):48-54. Erratum in: J Am Board Fam Pract 1999 Mar-Apr;12(2):187. PubMed PMID: 10050643.

6. Braddock CH 3rd, Fihn SD, Levinson W, Jonsen AR, Pearlman RA. How doctors and patients discuss routine clinical decisions. Informed decision making in the outpatient setting. J Gen Intern Med. 1997 Jun;12(6):339-45. PubMed PMID: 9192250.

7. Chalmers TC, Celano P, Sacks HS, Smith H Jr. Bias in treatment assignment in controlled clinical trials. N Engl J Med. 1983 Dec 1;309(22):1358-61. PubMed PMID: 6633598.

8. Chassin MR, Galvin RW, and the National Roundtable on Health Care Quality. The urgent need to improve health care quality: Institute of Medicine National Roundtable on Health Care Quality [consensus statement]. JAMA 1998;280(11):1000-1005. PMID: 9749483.

9. CMS: Centers for Medicare and Medicaid Services, Office of the Actuary, National Health Statistics Group, National Health Care Expenditures Data, January 2010.

10. Cohen SP. Epidural steroid injections for low back pain. BMJ. 2011 Sep 13;343:d5310. doi: 10.1136/bmj.d5310. PubMed PMID: 21914757.

11. Delfini Pre-Test Report at http://www.delfini.org/Delfini_Pre-Test_Report_0306.pdf

12. Echt DS, Liebson PR, Mitchell LB, et al. Mortality and morbidity in patients receiving encainide, flecainide, or placebo. The Cardiac Arrhythmia Suppression Trial. N Engl J Med. 1991 Mar 21;324(12):781-8. PubMed PMID: 1900101.

13. Eddy DM. Comparing benefits and harms: the balance sheet. JAMA. 1990 May 9;263(18):2493, 2498, 2501 passim. PubMed PMID: 2329639.

14. Eddy DM. Evidence-based medicine: a unified approach. Health Aff (Millwood). 2005 Jan-Feb;24(1):9-17. PubMed PMID: 15647211.

15. Freedman, David H. Lies, Damn Lies and Bad Medical Science. The Atlantic. November, 2010. www.theatlantic.com/magazine/archive/2010/11/lies-damned-lies-and-medical-science/8269/, accessed 11/07/2010.

16. Giannakakis IA, Haidich AB, Contopoulos-Ioannidis DG, Papanikolaou GN, Grilli R, Magrini N, Penna A, Mura G, Liberati A. Practice guidelines developed by specialty societies: the need for a critical appraisal. Lancet. 2000 Jan 8;355(9198):103-6. PubMed PMID: 10675167.

17. Glasziou P. The EBM journal selection process: how to find the 1 in 400 valid and highly relevant new research articles. Evid Based Med. 2006 Aug;11(4):101. PubMed PMID: 17213115.

18. Grilli R, Magrini N, Penna A, Mura G, Liberati A. Practice guidelines developed by specialty societies: the need for a critical appraisal. Lancet. 2000 Jan 8;355(9198):103-6. PubMed PMID: 10675167.

19. Guyatt GH, Oxman AD, Kunz R, Atkins D, Brozek J, Vist G, Alderson P, Glasziou P, Falck-Ytter Y, Schünemann HJ. GRADE guidelines: 2. Framing the question and deciding on important outcomes. J Clin Epidemiol. 2011 Apr;64(4):395-400. Epub 2010 Dec 30. PubMed PMID: 21194891.

20. Higgins JPT, Green S (editors). Cochrane Handbook for Systematic Reviews of Interventions Version 5.1.0 [updated March 2011]. The Cochrane Collaboration, 2011. Available from www.cochrane-handbook.org. Section 8.2.1. Accessed 11/9/12.

21. Ioannidis JPA. Why Most Published Research Findings are False. PLoS Med 2005; 2(8):696 701. PMID: 16060722.

22. IOM 2001: Institute of Medicine. Washington, D.C: National Academy Press; 2001. Crossing the Quality Chasm: A New Health System for the 21st Century.

23. IOM 2011: Guidelines: Institute of Medicine. 2011. Clinical Practice Guidelines We CanTrust. Washington, DC: The National Academies Press. Available at http://www.nap.edu/catalog.php?record_id=13058

24. Jefferson T, Demicheli V, Vale L. Quality of systematic reviews of economic evaluations in health care. JAMA. 2002 Jun 5;287(21):2809-12. PubMed PMID: 12038919.

25. Juni P, Altman DG, Egger M (2001) Systematic reviews in health care: assessing the quality of controlled clinical trials. BMJ 2001;323:42-6.PubMed PMID. 11440947.

26. Kerr EA, McGlynn EA, Adams J, Keesey J, Asch SM. Profiling the quality of care in twelve communities: results from the CEBCQI study. Health Aff. 2004;23(3):247-256. PMID: 15160823.

27. Kjaergard LL, Villumsen J, Gluud C. Reported methodological quality and discrepancies between large and small randomized trials in metaanalyses. Ann Intern Med 2001;135:982–89. PMID 11730399.

28. Kung J, Miller RR, Mackowiak PA. Failure of Clinical Practice Guidelines to Meet Institute of Medicine Standards: Two More Decades of Little, If Any, Progress. Arch Intern Med. 2012 Oct 22:1-6. doi: 10.1001/2013.jamainternmed.56. [Epub ahead of print] PubMed PMID: 23089902.

29. Lachin JM (filed as Lachin JL). Statistical considerations in the intent-to-treat principle. Control Clin Trials. 2000 Oct;21(5):526. PubMed PMID: 11018568. Erratum: Refers to John M. Lachin: http://www.sciencedirect.com/science/article/pii/S0197245600000921

30. Laine C, Taichman DB, Mulrow C. Trustworthy clinical guidelines. Ann InternMed. 2011 Jun 7;154(11):774-5. PubMed PMID: 21646561.

31. Lee BJ, Forbes K. The role of specialists in managing the health of populations with chronic illness: the example of chronic kidney disease. BMJ. 2009 Jul 8;339:b2395. doi: 10.1136/bmj.b2395. PubMed PMID: 19586983.

32. Leung. Modified by Delfini Group, LLC (www.delfini.org) from Leung GM. Evidence-based practice revisited. Asia Pac J Public Health. 2001;13(2):116-21. Review. PubMed PMID: 12597509.

33. Marciniak TA. Memorandum of June 14, 2010 on cardiovascular events in RECORD (NDA 21-071/S-035): FDA briefing document, pages 16-151. http://www.fda.gov/AdvisoryCommittees/Calendar/ucm214612.htm. Accessed July 9, 2010.

34. McGlynn EA, Asch SM, Adams J, et al. The quality of health care delivered to adults in the United States". N Engl J Med. 2003;348(26):2635-2645. PMID: 12826639.

35. McKibbon KA, Wilczynski NL, Haynes RB. What do evidence-based secondary journals tell us about the publication of clinically important articles in primary health care journals? BMC Med. 2004 Sep 6;2:33. PubMed PMID: 15350200.

36. Meinertz T, Zehender MK, Geibel A, Treese N, Hofmann T, Kasper W, Pop T. Long-term antiarrhythmic therapy with flecainide. Am J Cardiol. 1984 Jul 1;54(1):91-6. PubMed PMID: 6741844.

37. Mello MM, Brennan TA. The controversy over high-dose chemotherapy with autologous bone marrow transplant for breast cancer. Health Aff (Millwood). 2001 Sep-Oct;20(5):101-17. PubMed PMID: 11558695.

38. Moher D, Pham B, Jones A, Cook DJ, Jadad AR, Moher M, Tugwell P, Klassen TP. Does quality of reports of randomised trials affect estimates of intervention efficacy reported in meta-analyses? Lancet. 1998 Aug 22;352(9128):609-13. PubMed PMID: 9746022.

39. Morganroth J, Bigger JT Jr, Anderson JL. Treatment of ventricular arrhythmias by United States cardiologists: a survey before the Cardiac Arrhythmia Suppression Trial results were available. Am J Cardiol. 1990 Jan 1;65(1):40-8. PubMed PMID: 1688481.

40. NCEP: Report of the National Cholesterol Education Program Expert Panel on Detection, Evaluation, and Treatment of High Blood Cholesterol in Adults. The Expert Panel. Arch Intern Med. 1988 Jan;148(1):36-69. PubMed PMID: 3422148.

41. Owens DK, Lohr KN, Atkins D, Treadwell JR, Reston JT, Bass EB, Chang S, Helfand M. AHRQ series paper 5: grading the strength of a body of evidence when comparing medical interventions--agency for healthcare research and quality

and the effective health-care program. J Clin Epidemiol. 2010 May;63(5):513-23. PubMed PMID: 19595577.

42. Pitkin RM, Branagan MA, Burmeister LF. Accuracy of data in abstracts of published research articles. JAMA. 1999 Mar 24-31;281(12):1110-1. PubMed PMID:10188662.

43. Psaty BM, Prentice RL. Minimizing bias in randomized trials: the importance of blinding. JAMA. 2010 Aug 18;304(7):793-4. PubMed PMID: 20716744.

44. Reichenbach S, Sterchi R, Scherer M, Trelle S, Bürgi E, Bürgi U, Dieppe PA, Jüni P. Meta-analysis: chondroitin for osteoarthritis of the knee or hip. Ann Intern Med. 2007 Apr 17;146(8):580-90. PubMed PMID: 17438317.

45. Ruberman W, Weinblatt E, Goldberg JD, Frank CW, Shapiro S. Ventricular premature beats and mortality after myocardial infarction. N Engl J Med. 1977 Oct 6;297(14):750-7. PubMed PMID: 70750.

46. Sackett DL. Turning a blind eye: why we don't test for blindness at the end of our trials. BMJ. 2004 May 8;328(7448):1136. PubMed PMID: 15130997; PubMed Central PMCID: PMC406365.

47. Savovic J, Jones HE, Altman DG, et al. Influence of Reported Study Design Characteristics on Intervention Effect Estimates From Randomized, Controlled Trials. Ann Intern Med. 2012 Sep 4. doi: 10.7326/0003-4819-157-6-201209180-00537. [Epub ahead of print] PubMed PMID: 22945832.

48. Schulz KF, Chalmers I, Hayes RJ, Altman D. Empirical evidence of bias. Dimensions of methodological quality associated with estimates of treatment effects in controlled trials. JAMA 1995;273:408–12. PMID: 7823387.

49. Shaneyfelt TM, Centor RM. Reassessment of clinical practice guidelines: go gently into that good night. JAMA. 2009 Feb 25;301(8):868-9. PubMed PMID: 19244197.

50. Skinner J, Fisher ES, Wennberg JE; for the National Bureau of Economic Research. The efficiency of Medicare. Working Paper No. 8395. Cambridge, MA: National Bureau of Economic Research; July 2001.

51. Stone PW, Braccia D, Larson E. Systematic review of economic analyses of health care-associated infections. Am J Infect Control. 2005 Nov;33(9):501-9. Review. PubMed PMID: 16260325.

52. Straus SE, Ball C, Balcombe N, Sheldon J, McAlister FA. Teaching evidence-based medicine skills can change practice in a community hospital. J Gen Intern Med. 2005 Apr;20(4):340-3. PubMed PMID: 15857491.

53. Stuart ME, Handley MA, Chamberlain MA, Wallach RW, Penna PM, Stergachis A. Successful implementation of a guideline program for the rational use of lipid-lowering drugs. HMO Pract. 1991 Nov Dec;5(6):198-204. PubMed PMID:10115851.

54. van Tulder MW, Suttorp M, Morton S, et al. Empirical evidence of an association between internal validity and effect size in randomized controlled trials of low-back pain. Spine (Phila Pa 1976). 2009 Jul 15;34(16):1685-92. PubMed PMID: 19770609.

55. Windish DM, Huot SJ, Green ML. Medicine residents' understanding of the biostatistics and results in the medical literature. JAMA. 2007 Sep 5;298(9):1010-22. PMID: 17785646.

56. Young JM, Glasziou P, Ward JE. General practitioners' self ratings of skills in evidence based medicine: validation study. BMJ. 2002 Apr 20;324(7343):950-1. PubMed PMID: 11964341; PubMed Central PMCID: PMC102329.

INDEX

ABOUT THE AUTHORS

Delfini Group is a public service entrepreneurship founded to advance applied evidence- and value-based clinical quality improvements and methods through practice, training and facilitation. Much of Delfini's work is dedicated to help solve the little known societal problem of medical misinformation. Delfini has contributed to text books, advised government entities, worked with health care systems, payers and manufacturers and has trained thousands of health care professionals in evidence-based quality improvement.

Michael E. Stuart MD & Sheri Ann Strite are medical information scientists, medical evidologists and evidence-based clinical improvement experts who combine academic and practical experience to—

- Help health care systems apply evidence- and value-based clinical quality improvement methods including special help for work groups such as clinical guideline development teams, pharmacy & therapeutics and medical technology assessment committees, clinical quality improvement teams, journal clubs and more.

- Facilitate evidence-based clinical improvement projects.

- Create and/or facilitate the creation of clinical practice guidelines.

- Providing training in critical appraisal and medical decision-making project operations for leaders, staff and members including advanced seminars.

- Conduct evidence reviews and providing content for evidence-based projects.

- Train physicians and others in communicating with patients.

They have done extensive work with evidence-clinical quality improvement teams, medical technology assessment groups and Pharmacy & Therapeutics committees around the country.

Sheri Ann Strite, Co-founder, Principal & Managing Partner, initiated many Delfini health care improvement strategies, tools and training programs including the popular Delfini critical appraisal training program. Formerly she was Associate Director, Program Development, University of California, San Diego (UCSD) Family & Preventive Medicine, School of Medicine, where she taught faculty, physicians, residents, medical and pharmacy students and medical librarians. She was also a member of the UCSD Family Medicine Research Leaders and faculty for their Research Fellowship in the Department of Family & Preventive Medicine. Prior to UCSD, Ms. Strite worked in clinical improvement, education and research at Group Health Cooperative in Seattle, Washington, where she held various positions including leadership and research management and administration.

Michael E. Stuart MD, Co-founder, President & Medical Director, is a family physician and was appointed a clinical faculty position at the University of Washington in 1975. He is the former Director of the Department of Clinical Improvement and Education at Group Health Cooperative in Seattle, Washington, where he led development of more than 35 evidence-based clinical guidelines and other clinical improvements, chaired the Pharmacy & Therapeutics and Medical Technology Assessment Committees. His work has received praise from prominent health care leaders such as David Eddy MD, Don Berwick MD, Health Ministry of New Zealand and the US Navy Bureau of Medicine.

Topics upon which Delfini has written and taught include critical appraisal of medical literature, evidence-based committee processes, health care content development, technology assessment, population-based care, projecting economic and health outcomes, performance measurement, patient decision-making, facilitating provider behavior change, physician/patient communications, developing and implementing clinical guidelines, and creating information, decision and action aids for clinical care.

Strite and Stuart are authors of—

BASICS FOR EVALUATING MEDICAL RESEARCH STUDIES:
A Simplified Approach
And Why Your Patients Need You To Know This

Delfini Group Evidence-based Practice Series

Available at—
http://www.delfinigrouppublishing.com/

Editorial Reviews for *Basics for Evaluating Medical Research Studies:*

"Highly recommended! Sheri and Mike have distilled their many years of hands-on experience evaluating medical research and teaching others to do so into a succinct, practical and easy-to-understand handbook that clearly and simply explains to readers how to assess the quality and usefulness of clinical trials and other medical articles. Key statistical concepts are presented clearly and explained in a math-free way that is not intimidating. They also equip readers with a wealth of practical tools that have been refined over time into 1-page guides and checklists which are used by many around the world." **John C. Pezzullo, PhD, Biostatistician and Author of** *Biostatistics for Dummies*

"I am full of admiration for this terrific little book on evaluating medical research studies which is written clearly, simply and appropriately for a starter audience. Those with more experience often need reminding of the basics and can benefit from it too. I know of no other book that has succeeded so well in getting everything important covered so succinctly, which the authors have done brilliantly well!" **Richard Lehman, MA, BM, BCh,**

MRCGP, Senior Research Fellow, Oxford, and Blogger, *BMJ Journal Watch*

"This book provides a great introduction and guide for anyone who wants to understand how to interpret clinical research but feels intimidated by science or statistics. Sheri and Mike transform their experience of teaching these concepts to thousands of people into a format like they are speaking to you directly. For the evidologist there is a nice compilation of the evidence for critical appraisal components." **Brian S. Alper, MD, MSPH, FAAFP, Editor-in-Chief, DynaMed (dynamed.ebscohost.com)**

"This noteworthy book educates on many issues we address daily at **HealthNewsReview**.org. Written for physicians and other healthcare professionals, the authors write in terms the public can understand. Journalists who feed off a steady of diet of journal articles should read it along with the collection of tools at delfini.org. The book is only 112 pages. It won't overwhelm you, but will educate you on many of the themes we touch on so often as we analyze media messages about medical research studies. Strite and Stuart also provide examples to help educate." **Gary Schwitzer, Publisher, www.HealthNewsReview.org**